TEN OF THE BEST
BRITISH SHORT PLAYS

Previously published in the series

Ambiance/Almost Free Playscripts 1
Homosexual Acts: A Volume of Gay Plays

Ambiance/Almost Free Playscripts 3

TEN OF THE BEST
BRITISH SHORT PLAYS

Edited by ED Berman

**Inter-Action Inprint
London 1979**

First published in 1979 by Inter-Action Inprint,
15 Wilkin Street, London NW5 3NG

ISBN 0 904571 16 5 Hardback
ISBN 0 904571 17 3 Paperback

Typeset by T & R Filmsetters Limited,
77 Salusbury Road, London NW6 6NH

Printed and bound by Billing & Sons Limited,
Walnut Tree Close, Guildford, Surrey, U.K.

Contents

How Long Is an Ephemeron?

Looking back over ten years' ephemera — and by definition all live theatre is ephemeral — is like trying to trap quicksilver. Will these plays be less ephemeral when they are printed and published? After all, books seem to be more permanent than live theatre. Of course, to those in "the profession", everything else (including jobs as waiters or house cleaners) must seem more permanent.

Live theatre is currently trying to find a new costume in which to be seen and survive. This battle to survive against the appeal and compulsion of film, television and other leisure pursuits also has produced some interesting one-act plays. It may be the result of the conditioning influence of relatively short television time slots. Whatever it is, these plays seem to be of interest to wider and wider audiences. Unfortunately, though good one-act plays are easy to write, very good ones are difficult, and brilliant ones nearly impossible.

Our postman taught me this. Only he says that very bad ones must be easy to write because of the weight he delivers in the morning and the near equivalent weight he carries out each evening.

The phenomenon of transposing a short play written for one medium (radio or TV) into a stage version and vice-versa is becoming more frequent. The ephemera of one medium leap, in their attempt to live, to the most ephemeral platform of all — those tiny stages specialising in one-act plays.

In the 1968-78 decade in London, these stages have usually been lunchtime theatres. Most of the reasons for this are clear-cut, ranging from the small size of cast generally required, to the obvious one — the possibility of having your culture cake whilst eating it too.

The Ambiance Theatre Club began the permanent phase of the lunch-hour theatre movement by going into continuous production in 1968. At that time, the reasons for lunch-hour shows seemed to be more idealistic: people ought to be able to see theatre in more accessible and informal venues; theatre should fit into the normal daily pattern of a balanced working day; good professional shows ought to be less expensive than those found in palaces of high ceilings and other overheads; there should be showcases for "resting" actors to stretch their talents, a platform for budding writers and directors to get a start and for other experienced but stale theatre practitioners to rejuvenate themselves. Finally, experiments require both small studio theatres and low financial pressures to be genuine test-beds.

Did we survive because we achieved all of these objectives? Leaving theory aside, the simple truth is that we were lucky to have had a scandal over our first play. And what a scandal! Jennie Lee, a fine classical actress, was nude in a poetic reverie of a play, *Squire Jonathan* by John Arden — nude for three whole seconds.

In 1968 the Lord Chamberlain (that Star Chamber superstar of yesteryear) was still in business. His business was to censor plays and license them. We were a club theatre and unlicensed: thus we were defying the entire medieval power structure of the Establishment with a 3-second nude. What high drama! Thirty-five photographers showed up for the press photo-call. Subsequently we have had, on average, larger audiences without cameras.

As if this pathetic scandal were not enough, my own play, *The Nudist Campers Grow and Grow*, appeared next. A send-up of prudes, the play had two actors in fig-leaves defying the audience to join them on stage and shed their clothes. I am happy to say that few did. The flabbiness of the average bourgeois theatre-goer has to be seen to be believed.

By this time, The Arts Council of Great Britain decided to give us a tiny grant. Perhaps they felt that if we could afford costumes, we might cause less disruption of national customs.

Scandals aside, the original reasons for having theatre at lunch-time did have some substance to them. The lunch-hour venues *are* less formal (sometimes to the point of total discomfort). Ticket prices *are* a bargain, but no lunch-hour theatre (generally of a 50-seat capacity) could ever survive by box office bread alone.

Only with unemployed talent coming straight from the dole queue, or with generous Arts Council of Great Britain grants or local Council/

Regional Arts Association subsidy, can any of these necessary and vital "showcases" survive to fulfill any of the original expectations. With the growing pressure to unionize (coming not from Equity but from fringe theatres themselves), the subsidy factor has become absolutely essential.

The Ambiance, having made a break-through in obtaining a miniscule grant from the Arts Council in 1968, thus obtained credit. This allowed us to starve through to the next season. The small grant was in no way sufficient to account for survival. Perhaps, we survived because top playwrights and actors were willing to use this time slot to stretch themselves.

For example, Frank Marcus offered to let me direct his fine play, *The Window*, if I would accept Richard Pasco in the main role. After pondering for a split second I accepted. I thought I should set a condition, however, to show that experimental theatre practitioners had good business sense.

My condition was that I must be allowed to stage the play in a way that could not be reproduced on TV or film, uniquely using the environment of the stage/audience relationship. I thought that the play, set in a bedroom with its blind occupant desperate to "see" from the curtained window, should be staged so as to be seen through a curtained window by the audience. Frank doubted it could be done, unless I were willing to accept an audience of one Peeping Tom per show.

To solve this staging problem, I surrounded the set on three sides with muslin curtains. The audience filed in and sat with their backs to the walls some two feet away from the curtains through which they watched an extraordinary performance by Pasco of an extraordinary play by Marcus. The positioning of the seating enabled the audience to do what the blind character in the play wanted, desperately to do — truly to see into the life of the person next door without being seen.

This indoor variety of environmental theatre, where the audience is virtually a structural element in the set, has intrigued me over the years. It is difficult to find the perfect script for it, however. Often you simply have to settle for being able to watch a fine play through a traditional fourth wall. This is, in itself, a great pleasure. If only you can find the play to produce such pleasure and stimulation.

The Ambiance has survived to its Tenth Anniversary through two bankruptcies — not ours, the restauranteurs', our Landlords. Restaurants only invite you to use their facilities if they cannot fill their space and if they think you'll bring them trade. This is a classic case of not having a cake so let's eat it for two.

At the time of the first bankruptcy of the Ambiance Restaurant we took to the streets with James Saunders' *Dog Accident*, previously a radio play, set in a busy street at lunch-time. I had wanted to do it in its appropriate venue in any case. The restauranteur didn't have to go bankrupt to reinforce my environmental tendencies. We were going to use a real dog for this play, but couldn't find a dead one that looked real enough. Finally, we used a wired-up stuffed dog, radio controlled, that twitched and screamed when I twiddled a dial some twenty yards away — a very special effect by the man who had created the special effects for the Battle of Britain film.

Having lost the original Ambiance Restaurant, our next temporary home was the Green Banana Restaurant. Before it went the way of all good green bananas, we produced the premiere of Tom Stoppard's *After Magritte*. Tom was attracted to us, I think, by the whole idea of Inter-Action — both the theatre and community sides. Letting us do his play was a gift beyond the call of curiosity, however.

The Green Banana was a basement restaurant measuring 14ft. x 25ft. with a pillar in the middle (for a world premiere, no less). Every morning at 5.00 a.m. during the run of *After Magritte* a removal lorry would pull up outside the restaurant in the empty Frith Street of Soho. By that time of night everyone else seemed to have finally found a stage on which to rehearse their own branch of the entertainment industry.

The pieces of the box set of *After Magritte* would emerge from the lorry. Stacked on the pavement, the pieces waited. Then the entire contents of the Green Banana, basement night club extraordinaire, were carried up to the street and loaded into the lorry. Next the pieces of the set were carried down the narrow winding stair by two dedicated Stage Managers. These tortuous acrobatics completed, the set was ensconced for lunch by 11.00 a.m.

The lorry, now far out of danger from marauding meter maids, would wait patiently three miles away in a free parking zone. Its job was to return the restaurant props (tables, chairs, chandeliers, ever-empty cash register, etc.) by 2.15 p.m. after the lunch-time performance. This would guarantee that the reverse transformation back to a night club-restaurant could take place in time for the small·but select dinner clientele.

After this production, a slight change seemed to creep into Stoppard's demeanour whenever we met. It might have meant, "Do you own shares in lorry companies?" This inaccurate but not insane suspicion of his was unfortunately reinforced when I asked 150 British artists to help me fill the Fun Art Bus with a zany potpourri of music, theatre, films, poetry and pleasure. The bus, a transformed London double decker, had the smallest proscenium arch theatre in the world installed on the upper deck. To be appropriate, I needed smallish plays to fit into this moving theatrical experience.

Stoppard, seemingly hooked on the now indisputable connection between the motor industry and the theatre world, fulfilled the commission perfectly — a 15-minute edition of *Hamlet* for seven actors. We both coincidentally misplaced the script for four years, though the bus soldiered on courageously without any resolution of its existential predicament — to be a bus or not to be.

Four years later, in 1976, the Fun Art Bus stopped outside the new National Theatre of Great Britain on a journey from an adventure playground. It had just delivered four performances to the children of Southwark, by our children's theatre company, Prof. Dogg's Troupe. The Bus, without envy, watched the Dogg's Troupe perform Stoppard's *Hamlet* on the grey parapets of the National Theatre.

To date, the National Theatre is the largest theatre set I have ever had built for a one-act play. (The theatre mind wanders into reality: Is the National Theatre of Great Britain really Elsinore in disguise?) A thousand people a day could, and did, watch a matinee or evening performance of this *Hamlet* between 5.15 p.m. and 6.30 p.m., before they wandered with premonition into the plush interior of Elsinore to see the longer version.

The name of Dogg's Troupe is derived from my pseudonym as a writer for children, Prof. R. L. Dogg. I had not written anything for children at that time but, in case I did, I wanted to have a suitable name.

Furthermore, I adopted this name in order to try to amuse dry academics who leaf through library index cards in their never-ending search for permanence. I have no better purpose in life than bringing cheer to this alienated and deprived sector of our community; I wished to do this from a distance, however. In the index they would someday find my children's doggerel rhymes listed under Dogg, R.L.

When told this simple explanation for an even simpler pseudonym, Stoppard said anyone who could wait that long for a bad pun to explode deserved better. So he wrote *Dogg's Our Pet*: the title is an anagram of Dogg's Troupe, which is itself an imperfect homonym. I've always marvelled at how simple comedy can be when you analyse it!

A script as good as that usually comes about through commissioning only, and there are few writers who accept commissions of green bananas. Truly fine scripts seem to appear only once out of 500 unsolicited ones brought daily to the office with a gentle grimace by the head-shaking postman.

One such script was *Have You Met Our Rabbit?*, a remarkable first play by Michael Stevens. Paired with *Dogg's Our Pet*, it was the opening double-bill (December 1971) in our new theatre, The Almost Free.

Having lost the original Ambiance Restaurant and its next temporary home, the Green Banana Restaurant, the theatre club went for a season each to the ICA and the Oval House. Following this, the final move (or what seemed to be the final move) was to The Almost Free Theatre. This theatre of Inter-Action's was purpose-renovated from an electric bingo hall in the West End of London, two streets from Piccadilly Circus.

The Almost Free derives its name from its box office policy of pay-what-you-can (at least 1p.) and its experimental artistic policy of new plays only. At least that's the reasoning.

The fact is that I had been arguing with three of my associate directors, Jim Hiley, Roland Rees and Naftali Yavin, about the concept and title of a "Free Theatre".

I went up to the blackboard we were using for brainstorming and wrote "The Free Theatre". A row broke out with the others claiming the Arts Council would never let us get away with having no income from the box office. "All right," I said, always willing to compromise when I see I will lose a vote. So I wrote "Almost" on the board just above "The Free Theatre" and walked out of the room. That tactic always ends arguments — temporarily.

In the second season at The Almost Free Theatre (March 1972) we produced *The Ragpickers* by Norman Smythe, under the brilliant direction of the late Naftali Yavin. This showed me a realism and naturalism on stage that I thought possible only by going to the streets.

Sometimes friends send you scripts: like Heathcote William's *Hancock's Last Half Hour* which was still touring two years after opening in April 1976.

Hancock's Last Half Hour (65 minutes) was similar to Stoppard's *Dirty Linen* (85 minutes) in the sense that although originally performed as a longish lunch-time show, it has managed to shift to evening venues without complaints from audiences about its shortish length. (Perhaps this is proof of the conditioning power of television time slots.)

Heathcote forgot he had sent the play to us. So he sent a copy to the National Theatre as well. We agreed to do the play and the National also wanted it. Heathcote was invited to see a show at the National where they wined and dined him in the VIP room anxiously trying to persuade him to let them do the play in their splendid foyer as an early evening attraction. You will remember that this foyer had doubled as the Green Room in my FIsinore set in Stoppard's 15 minute *Hamlet*. (It is a useful foyer, well worth the hundreds of thousands spent on it!)

Heathcote, so he tells it, had been half convinced (or tipsy?) before he went back in to see the second act of the evening's production at the National. As the curtain went up, it didn't. That is to say, at the Lyttleton that evening (with paraphenalia controlled by tens of thousands of pounds worth of modern equipment) the curtain got stuck three feet from the floor. Exit Heathcote Williams not wanting to work with a theatre that couldn't pull itself up by its own bootstraps.

Thus, we got the rights to the play that has been our most successful touring production ever, after playing for months at The Almost Free. It could go on tour for forty weeks a year forever, if we could find an actor who wanted to do it for that long a run.

On another tack, finding pieces of writing that have never been done as plays and making them work on stage is a great pleasure. Perhaps it ought to be called theatre trouvé.

Pinter's remarkable short story *The Examination* (15 minutes) is such a piece. When spoken on stage directly, without pauses except for breathing, it produced an electric shock during our Rights and Campaigns season in 1978.

Also in this season, Inter-Action Productions presented *The Irish Hebrew Lesson* by Wolf Mankowitz. Perhaps our most successful play to date in terms of reviews, box office, and attendance, it will undoubtedly be seen for many years to come in many languages. In its story and language(s), the play expresses a universality and cry for peace without ever making a didactic statement about either.

So many of the 500 plays that weary the postman's shoulders weary the playreader's soul. Preaching has already driven most churches out of business. Why don't young playwrights stop going to church on a typewriter. It's an altogether unholy waste of time on everyone's part. Sermonizing is for empty pews. The nature of theatre abhors that vacuum.

The use of a seasonal theme has been a characteristic of the Ambiance. Quite often the theme has been of dubious provenance. Three new plays by left-handed writers and three others by right-handed ones could be called "Left v. Right". Usually though we have been able to plan far ahead and to spend time searching out plays to fit themes as opposed to concocting themes to fit a random set of plays. Thematic threads through three or more plays in a season can give an artistic director the opportunity to present the questioning of important issues from different points of view for the audience.

Some of our most successful seasons have been: Black and White Power Plays; Homosexual Acts; The Women's Season; and Rights and Campaigns. Each of these seasons has launched, by intention, another theatre company to pursue its own self-expression as a libertarian group.

The structure and organization of theatre is often more important than what any single play purports to say on stage. Words are not social action and staged words rarely if ever lead to action. But organized groups of people, whose reasons for organizing extend beyond the fourth wall, can be an opening wedge to be reckoned with. They must, however, use their organization to extend the principles of their messages into reality. The dramatic words do not set an example nor do they even give much of a lead to others. The actions, beyond script and role, outside suspended disbelief, are proof of the meaning of the dialogue. The movement from belief to action is an emerging role of modern theatre.

For it is in its difference from TV and films that theatre must find its role. The impossible competition of the media in the areas of theatre's traditional roles of storytelling and holding a mirror up to reality forces such a change. The mirror of theatre has been eclipsed by the silver screen and the non-reflecting tube.

Live theatre will now look to its assets to find its survival:
- that it can use and change its environment at the point of playing
- that it can respond to the audience
- that it can allow the audience to respond and, in turn, change itself accordingly
- that it can physically and verbally involve the audience
- that it involves the risk of accident by being live

Perhaps most important of all is that theatre, because of its live confrontation potential, can create a sense of event or can be an event — a celebration of, or an attack on reality.

Lunch-hour theatre is hardly the epitome of this crystal-ball gazing. It is one of the modest ways in which dozens of theatre companies in the last few years in Britain have sought to find new directions — socially, politically, financially, structurally and even aesthetically.

By the nature of the relatively small size of theatre audiences, theatre becomes exclusive. Theatre is for this reason the wrong place to claim political influence. In the modern state, where theatre is subsidized by the taxpayer, modesty should prevail in our medieval guild of craftsmen.

The extraordinary privilege of being paid to express ourselves to
limited numbers of our paymasters is an enviable position in our
world. We should remember that it fills neither sufficient bodies nor
souls to claim a shattering social or political role.

In any case, there will always be something special, though not
necessarily good, about those events in life such as theatre
performances, which pretend to higher things in small packages.
These experiences are events which cannot be repeated because they
were alive, even though the words of the script can be repeated. By
being a special event, each theatre piece is an "ephemeron". Its
value lies in passing on emotional charge without visible trace.

ED Berman
London, 1978.

The Window
by Frank Marcus

The first stage performance of *The Window* was at the original Ambiance Lunch-Hour Theatre Club at the Ambiance Restaurant, London W2, on the 4th February 1969, with:

 Richard Pasco, OBE
 David Cook
 Warwick Stuart

An Inter-Action Production designed and directed by ED Berman

Approximate playing time: 40 minutes

PHOTOGRAPH: MORRIS NEWCOMBE

The bedroom and ante-room of a small, modern flat. An early evening in June.

A pleasant glow of sunshine comes from a window. The window is open, and the curtains are slightly agitated by the breeze. There is a door leading to the kitchen and one leading to an ante-room.

When the curtain rises, RICHARD TREMAYNE *is discovered sitting in bed, propped up against his pillows, smoking a cigarette through a holder. The transistor radio by his side is switched on, playing the overture to "Orpheus in the Underworld".*

There is a buzz from the front door, followed almost immediately by the sound of a key turning in the lock. KEN *enters the ante-room. He is a small, youngish man in a raincoat, carrying a carrier-bag.*

KEN *(calling)* Mr. Tremayne? Are you there, sir?

TREMAYNE *(switching off the radio)* Hello! Come in, this way.

> KEN *enters the bedroom*

I've been expecting you.

KEN I'm sorry I'm a bit late, sir. Ralph didn't tell me until Tuesday . . .

TREM No need to apologize. Make yourself at home. There's a plate of this frozen food stuff in the fridge. I think you'll find everything you want.

KEN Thank you, sir.

> *He goes into the kitchen*

TREM *(calling after him)* You'll find a can of beer there, too. Ralph got that in specially.

KEN *(from the kitchen)* Thank you. Yes, I can see it. *(He busies himself in the kitchen)*

> *Pause.*

TREM *(calling)* I say!

2

KEN	*(appearing in the kitchen door)* Yes, sir?
TREM	I don't know your name.

KEN *enters the bedroom*

KEN	Oh, it's Ken, sir. I've known Ralph for some time. We were in the army . . .
TREM	I see. *(After a pause)* Ralph's been with me for nearly four years, you know.
KEN	Yes, he often talks about you.
TREM	Not in a derogatory way, I hope.
KEN	*(embarrassed)* Oh, no, sir. Far from it . . .
TREM	I was only joking.
KEN	*(after a pause)* Have you eaten, sir?
TREM	Yes, thank you. Ralph always brings in dinner, before he goes out. Just look after yourself; don't worry about me.

> KEN *goes back to the kitchen, and* TREMAYNE
> *switches on the wireless again.* KEN, *carrying a
> plate in his hands, stands uncertainly in the
> doorway.*

Did you want something?

> KEN, *startled, nearly drops the plate*

You didn't think I could see you.

KEN	It wasn't that, sir . . .
TREM	*(switching off the radio again)* Most people are surprised at the way I — sense where they are. You see, when one is blind, one develops one's other faculties to a very marked degree. I can almost — don't laugh — I can almost exactly visualize what you look like. By the way, do sit down by that little table and have your dinner. You see, I have a highly developed imagination.
KEN	That's — very interesting. *(He sits down in the small chair,*

3

and starts eating) What do I look like, then? Let's hear the worst.

TREM   You are smallish — I can hear that from the direction of your voice: you are quite plump, I should say.

KEN   *(laughing)* I could do with losing a few pounds!

TREM   Obviously, you must be about Ralph's age — twenty-eight?

KEN   Twenty-nine, actually. Still, that's near enough.

TREM   I see you with brown, curly hair, with a sort of quiff — you know, a small cascade, in the middle . . .

KEN   *(involuntarily putting his hand to his hair)* I say, I'm beginning to think you're pretending to be blind.

TREM   *(with a slight nervous laugh)* Yes, that's what many of them think. And you have a face like a coconut.

KEN   A coconut?

TREM   Please, don't take offence. I am in the habit of thinking of faces in terms of animals, plants, or fruit. The second I heard you I knew you had a fruit face. It was just a question of deciding . . .

KEN   I don't know whether to be flattered, or what.

TREM   Coconuts are excellent: firm, nourishing, exotic really. Cigarette?

KEN   *(rising and helping himself from the box beside the bed)* Thank you, sir.

TREM   Meal all right?

KEN   Yes, thank you, sir. *(He sits again)*

TREM   There's a tin of fruit salad . . .

KEN   I'll have that later, if I may, sir.

TREM   As you wish.

4

KEN	May I ask you a question, sir?
TREM	Certainly, by all means.
KEN	If you're so good at guessing, or sensing, all this about people, why don't you get about a bit more? I mean, it would do you good to get out a bit. Lying in here, all cooped up . . .
TREM	Don't you like this flat?
KEN	Oh, no, it's not that! It's a lovely flat; very cosy, really, and convenient, I should say . . .

        Pause

TREM	*(thoughtfully puffing on his cigarette)* The accepted thing to do is to try to overcome one's disabilities, eh? After all, there's some little thing wrong with almost everybody . . .
KEN	I can't say I've ever looked at it in this light. Of course, I used to do a bit of nursing.
TREM	A male nurse?
KEN	I was never qualified, or anything. Just used to help out in an old people's home. And nowadays I look after my mother; she's bedridden, too.
TREM	*(quietly)* So Ralph has left me in competent hands . . .
KEN	I'll do my best, sir.
TREM	He told you, I take it?
KEN	*(quickly)* Yes, sir.
TREM	And — what did you think?
KEN	Look, I'm here to do a job, to help out an old friend. It's not my place to probe into what people do, or want, or anything. As long as it's not illegal . . .
TREM	Admirable sentiments.

KEN	Would you like me to read to you, sir? The papers, or anything?
TREM	*(picking up a book from the table beside him)* You can read me a page of this. I got as far as "Groundsel".
KEN	*(rising and taking the book)* The Oxford Dictionary! Are you interested in words, then? I used to go to evening classes at the Polytechnic . . .
TREM	"Groundsel."
KEN	*(reading)* "Groundsel. Archaic. Timber serving as foundation, lowest part of wooden framework; threshold. Next: Group. Fine Arts: two or more figures or objects forming complete design or distinct part of one . . ."
TREM	Stop! I can't — I can't bear it!
KEN	Anything wrong, sir? Are you in pain?
TREM	*(shaking his head)* No, no, it will pass. *(After a pause)* Sit down there, Ken. Make yourself comfortable. *(He indicates the small chair)*
KEN	*(sitting)* If there's anything you want . . .
TREM	It was the sound of your voice — I was trying to get used to it. After all, you'll have to do a lot of talking, afterwards. I want everything kept quite impersonal, you understand? I shall want you to report quite unemotionally what you see, unadorned by sentiment or inhibition.
KEN	*(nervously)* Yes, I know. Ralph told me.
TREM	*(after a pause)* What time is it?
KEN	Just on seven, sir.
TREM	Good. That should give us another clear half hour. You seem to be a sensitive sort of chap, Ken. I think I shall tell you something about the background of this whole — thing. To try to make you understand.

KEN	That's very kind of you, sir, but I am really not at all curious. I'll just do what you ask me to do, without getting personally involved.
TREM	Have you ever been in love?

> KEN *does not reply*

	You consider this question as prying? Don't be afraid to tell me.
KEN	Well, yes, sir, I don't really see it's got anything to do . . .
TREM	Your innermost feelings are your own, eh? An impenetrable citadel. Splendid.
KEN	Well, I'm not asking <u>you</u> anything, so it's only fair . . .
TREM	Be quiet, you are being impertinent. *(Losing his temper)* You can leave, if you like! I can manage without you, or Ralph, or anybody! Get out, you smug bastard! Do you hear me — get out!
KEN	*(rising; pale and anxious)* I haven't said nothing!
TREM	*(trembling)* Give me a light.

> KEN *quickly holds a match to* TREMAYNE's *cigarette*

	I'm sorry. I'm sorry — forgive me.
KEN	*(relieved)* That's all right, sir. Don't worry. It's just that you're a bit on edge, like. It's not really surprising, after all you've been through.
TREM	Sit down. Are you quite comfortable?
KEN	Oh, yes, perfectly, sir. *(He sits again)*
TREM	Please, stop calling me "sir".
KEN	As you wish, s . . ., Mr Tremayne. Would you like me to go on with the reading?
TREM	No, thank you, Ken. Just sit still, and listen.

KEN   I'm listening, Mr Tremayne.

TREM   I lost my sight in a car crash — Ralph will no doubt have told you . . .

KEN   A most unfortunate accident.

TREM   It was no accident. I had meant to kill myself. Does that shock you? It was in Cornwall — quite near where I was born. It seemed fitting to me, in keeping with my sense of style, that I should end where I began. It would have made an artistic whole.

KEN   *(quietly)* I am sorry, sir.

TREM   *(bitterly)* Your sympathy is entirely misplaced. Imagine for a moment — no, seriously, try to imagine — what makes a man attempt suicide. I had to die — there was no other choice. For weeks I struggled to find an acceptable alternative — no good! Like a feared, but familiar face, death smiled at me from the darkness. Once I accepted it, I felt relieved, almost at peace. My time was taken up with devising intricate ways of ending my life. Nothing hasty, nothing sordid; something that would sum up neatly my endeavours and my ideals. In the end I decided to crash my car through the sea-wall at dawn. I fixed the exact spot — a spot that held the most pleasurable recollections for me. By crashing there, I would destroy, but also in a way perpetuate, this recollection.

KEN   Might I ask what kind of recollection it was? If you'd rather not . . .

TREM   That's perfectly all right: you are entitled to know. It was the spot directly in front of a beach hut rented annually by my parents. One day I heard a voice just below me, from the beach. It was a child's voice. She was squatting down, her legs like matchsticks, talking to herself while arranging pebbles and sea-shells in neat rows. I couldn't see her face — she had her back to me. "Only the blinding glory of her long fair hair, reflecting in the sun." I returned to the hut, thinking nothing more of it. *(He puffs at his cigarette)* A week or so later, I saw her again. She came running up to the hut, tear-stained, heart-broken.

"Please, please," she implored me, "my beach ball is floating away on the waves. It was all new — a birthday present!" I ran down to the sea. The beach ball seemed quite close, lightly riding the waves. I swam out after it, as fast as I could. Every time I came within grasping distance of it, it eluded me, by slipping away over an incoming wave. There it was: glistening brightly in the sun. I can see it now: red, white, yellow, and green stripes. I must have swum after it for a long time — longer than was good for me. The next thing I remember was hearing the child's voice again. "Please, don't die, please don't die," she kept repeating, like an incantation. I remember thinking: "How funny, whoever wants to die?" I opened my eyes. I was lying on the beach, and there was a small group of people standing around me, staring at me. It appears that I had lost consciousness in the water, and a boat had got to me just in time and picked me up. My first words were: "Where's the ball?" "What ball, what ball?" she said, uncomprehending. I scanned the horizon — there was the beach ball: a tiny black spot, gently bobbing up and down. If I had died that day, everything would have been perfect . . .

KEN   *(rising)* One never knows. It's not right to say things like that . . .

TREM   Are you religious?

        KEN *does not reply*

You're lucky, really lucky. I could never manage it, and I tried hard.

KEN   *(after a pause)* Was that the — young lady . . .?

TREM   *(lost in reminiscence)* I referred to her jokingly as "my would-be murderess". We became really good friends, although I was twice her age . . .

        A clock strikes

It's half past; we must get ready!

KEN   Where shall I sit?

TREM   *(indicating the window)* In that armchair. You'll find the binoculars at the side, on the window-sill.

9

KEN goes to the window-sill and picks up a pair of binoculars

KEN — I've got them, sir. *(He sits in the armchair)*

TREM — Quite comfortable?

KEN — Yes, thank you.

TREM — The glasses were adjusted to Ralph's requirements. I believe he has normal eyesight.

KEN — So have I, thank God.

TREM — Train them carefully now on the ground-floor opposite, the fourth window from the left. Have you got that?

KEN — Yes, I have got that. *(Relieved)* There's nothing to be seen.

TREM — Describe the furniture.

KEN — Well, it's just an ordinary living-room: sideboard, dining table, chairs . . .

TREM — Television?

KEN — Yes, in the corner . . .

TREM — You are wrong: there is no television.

KEN — *(stuttering)* Well, what is it, then? It looks like . . .

TREM — My poor Ken. You are short-sighted! Go on, lad, try again: adjust your binoculars. Go on.

KEN — *(looking very hard)* It's a sort of — of cupboard.

TREM — *(sighing with relief)* That's better. You mustn't think me pedantic, Ken, but exactitude of observation is essential in these matters.

KEN — I quite appreciate that.

TREM — Can you distinguish the picture above the sideboard?

KEN — *(quickly)* Yes, it's a face: a clown's face.

10

TREM	Good! Yes, it's a Rouault print I gave her for her twenty-first birthday . . .

Pause

KEN	There's nobody in there.
TREM	There wouldn't be, just yet. Maybe another twenty minutes or so. Keep looking, though. Don't shift your glance for a single moment — you must tell me the minute you see anything.
KEN	You can rely on me, Mr. Tremayne.
TREM	Help yourself to another cigarette.
KEN	Not just yet, sir, thank you.
TREM	How strange to think that you are about to see her for the very first time, and you're not even excited by the prospect.
KEN	But I <u>am</u>, sir, I'm really curious . . .
TREM	*(sharply)* Don't turn to speak to me — keep looking!
KEN	Sorry.
TREM	Do you believe in love at first sight? Don't answer. Of course, I had known her as a child; then, for almost five years, I lost touch with her. I sometimes thought of her — remembering her as a child. It never occurred to me that she must have grown up.
KEN	How did you meet her again?
TREM	By a complete coincidence. I had arranged to meet a friend at the theatre. He told me he'd bring a girl, but I had no idea who she would be. They were late. The national anthem was played — still no sign of them. The house-lights dimmed, the curtain rose. The play was "Twelfth Night" — a miserable, stilted performance. Suddenly, very softly, hardly noticeably, I felt someone occupying the seat next to mine. I didn't even look. Then a very quiet voice: "Sorry we were late — my fault, I'm afraid." I turned. I didn't recognize her in the dark, but she immediately recognized

me. From the moment she looked at me, she never took her eyes off me. I could feel them on me throughout the performance: I felt quite embarrassed, and ashamed for my friend. Large, blue eyes, at the same time liquid and steely. Extraordinary eyes. Then, suddenly, she whispered to me: "Please, don't die; please, don't die." *(He is very moved by the recollection)* Why did you say that, my darling, in that tone of voice? It's what Beauty says to the Beast in the fairy-tale. What would you say to me now, my beloved, if you knew? *(After a long pause)* Anyone there yet?

KEN   No sir, not yet. I haven't stopped looking.

TREM   You know, as one gets older, recollections can really hurt — in a physical way, I mean. I don't know what it is about one's youth that one misses so much: I think it is the quality of hope. Time never seems pressing — the future seems vast and promising. All one's ambitions and ideals seem fulfillable. Calamities are merely pebbles in one's path. The look she gave me that night in the darkened auditorium made my heart jump. I had the complete certainty that perfection was at hand . . .

KEN   *(sighing)* I know just how you must have felt, sir.

TREM   *(interested)* Really? You, too, have felt . . .

KEN   Many a time.

TREM   Tell me about it.

KEN   I can't, sir. You mustn't get angry, but I really can't express these things. Anyway, I should think most people have these high hopes at one time or another; if they didn't, hardly anybody would ever get married, now would they?

TREM   You don't like women, do you?

             There is no reply

         Don't be ashamed to tell me; I am quite unshockable. We all have our little idiosyncracies . . .

             KEN *gets up, and angrily puts the binoculars on the window-sill*

	Ken, what have you done? *(Very worried)* What — are you doing?
KEN	I don't know what I'm doing here. *(Moving below the bed to the door)* I should never have come.
TREM	Get back to this chair! You can't leave me now — it's nearly time.
KEN	I told you I didn't want to get personally involved . . .
TREM	*(apologetically)* Yes, I know. I shouldn't have questioned you. I am really, deeply sorry. I have so little contact with people; I tend to get curious — not in any morbid way, I assure you. Please, stay, Ken, I beg you. I am completely in your hands: I entirely rely on you.
KEN	Why did you say that, then, about me?
TREM	I wanted to find out how you would look at her. I am pleased, really pleased, that you — are what you are. I like the commentary to be truly dispassionate, untainted . . .
KEN	In that case, why did you tell me all these stories, all this past history?
TREM	Because I wanted you to understand. My God, <u>don't</u> you understand? I have asked you to come here to do something that most people would regard as perverted, if not obscene: something morally reprehensible. By explaining to you, I tried to make you realize that what you are asked to do is not degrading, but part of an expression of love: a love without which I cannot live. The last remaining reason for my existence. Please, please, go back.
KEN	*(moving back to the armchair)* All right, Mr Tremayne. If it's something you need . . .
TREM	Have you got the glasses? *(Anxiously)* Are they adjusted?
KEN	*(after giving Tremayne a long look, and shaking his head)* I'm focusing them now.
TREM	Well? Well, is anyone there? Why don't you speak? Has she come in?

KEN	*(steadily)* She has just come in, sir.
TREM	*(to himself)* Thank God, thank God. Tell me, tell me everything!
KEN	There's not much to tell, really. She's just sort of — tidying up.
TREM	What is she wearing? What does she look like? What do you think of her, Ken? Isn't she beautiful? Honestly now, as an impartial observer, have I exaggerated?
KEN	She's a very nice looking girl, sir.
TREM	Yes — yes. Is she wearing her hair up or down?
KEN	She's wearing it up. She's just put on a house-coat, or dressing-gown, is it?
TREM	It's a dressing-gown. She has never owned a house-coat. She would regard that with contempt — women's magazine stuff. What is she doing?
KEN	Still tidying — papers and stuff.
TREM	Does she seem happy? Is she singing to herself?
KEN	She's gone to the kitchen — but that window's got curtains up.
TREM	Yes, I know. I know. She's probably preparing a meal. She usually has — someone round for dinner on Thursday night. I wonder who it'll be? And not only Thursdays. I'd better tell you, Ken, she has men calling on her. Regularly, you understand?
KEN	I understand.
TREM	Ralph knows them all by sight — he has nicknames for each of them.
KEN	Do the same ones always call on the same evenings?
TREM	Oh, yes, they are — regular clients . . .

KEN	It's a shame, really, isn't it, sir, that a nice girl . . .
TREM	It had to happen. It was inevitable. It was in her nature. Nobody could have saved her — I realize that now . . .
KEN	She's come back again. Looks like she's laying the table for dinner . . .
TREM	You see — I told you!
KEN	Dinner for two. A cosy little party . . .
TREM	Can you see her face? It should be quite clear: it's still light, isn't it?
KEN	Yes, I can see her clearly.
TREM	She's not beautiful, certainly not in a classical sense. Do you know what I used to like best about her face? Liked, you know, rather than admired? You will laugh — her nostrils! I used to say they were curved as delicately as those of a Dresden shepherdess. Can you see her?
KEN	She's gone to the sideboard — wineglasses?
TREM	That's her attempt at gracious living. Nothing must ever be sordid. Although some of the men who call on her . . .
KEN	You can't always go by appearances.
TREM	I don't. But, sometimes, you know, they go to her bedroom — and in the heat of the moment forget to draw the curtains.
KEN	*(shocked)* Surely Ralph doesn't . . .
TREM	He tells me everything. Detailed descriptions. You see, I have to know the truth.
KEN	I should have thought there were some things . . .
TREM	*(sharply)* You are not here to think. What is she doing now?
KEN	*(slowly)* She's making herself look pretty. I expect he's due any moment.

TREM   She's combing her hair?

KEN   At the moment, she's putting on some lipstick.

TREM   I wish she wouldn't do that. All the time we were together,
          she never used any make-up. It just wasn't necessary.
          Her mouth is beautifully shaped; she has a very well-defined
          upper lip. She had a habit of sucking it in when she had
          done something wrong. It made her look so childish and
          vulnerable that one instantly forgave her — it was
          completely disarming.

KEN   *(announcing)* He's arrived.

TREM   What? Who has arrived?

KEN   The man. The visitor.

TREM   Who is it? What does he look like?

KEN   A young man — nice looking, really. One of those casual
          suede jackets — Italian, I think they are.

TREM   It must be Gerald. That's the name Ralph gave him.

KEN   That's the one — I mean, he looks like a "Gerald".

TREM   Please, confine your observations to what you see.

KEN   Well, they greeted each other very cordially — a nice hug,
          you know. He brought her a box — chocolates, would
          it be?

TREM   Most probably. Yes, he's one of the . . . better-mannered
          ones. Gerald. Funny, I almost approve of Gerald. The sort
          of innocuous young man she might have married, if . . .

KEN   I don't think you would approve if you saw them now!

TREM   What — what are they doing?
                    KEN *sniggers*
          Speak, blast you!

16

TREM	The light on?
KEN	No light; there's nothing to be seen.
TREM	Give me a cigarette.

> KEN *hands him a cigarette and lights a match for him*

Thank you. I ought to be used to it by now. It happens as regularly as clockwork. The same meaningless actions, again and again.

KEN	I don't suppose it's meaningless to the parties concerned.
TREM	That's where you are wrong. The moment it's over, it becomes meaningless.
KEN	Yes, but while it lasts . . .
TREM	*(icily)* Get back to your chair, and watch, and report when you see something. *(He switches on the radio and smokes his cigarette in silence)*

> KEN *goes back to the armchair*

KEN	*(with a smile on his face)* It is darkening. Soon I won't be able to distinguish anything.
TREM	*(lost in thought)* What did you say? *(He turns off the radio)*
KEN	Nothing. Nothing of importance.

> *There is a long pause*

TREM	Every time it's the same: the same anxiety, the same tension, the same despair . . . *(Softly, to himself)* There's no shirking it: I must imagine it all. Every gesture, every look, every breath she takes . . . What am I hoping for? A miracle? That she will suddenly call my name? Loud enough for me to hear across the courtyard?
KEN	There's no sign of any activity, sir. *(He gives an embarrassed laugh)*
TREM	In the fairy-tale, the Beast is saved in the nick of time. Maybe one has to go to the very limit — to hold a knife to

KEN	Well, it's getting rather intimate. They're on the settee. She's lying across his lap.
TREM	*(after a pause)* Go on!
	KEN *does not reply*
	Go on!
KEN	I'd have thought, with your highly-developed imagination . . .
TREM	Please, Ken. Please. I didn't mean to antagonize you. I must know — can't you understand?
KEN	Oh, all right.
TREM	Well? He's unbuttoned her blouse?
KEN	She's taken if off. He's kissing her . . . all over.
	TREMAYNE *hurls the dictionary in the direction of* KEN
	Steady, sir. *(He jumps up)* That could have hurt me, if it had landed on my head.
TREM	*(choked with anger)* It was aimed at her! Every day of the week she betrays me. Why does she do it? I gave her everything . . . *(He buries his face in his pillows, shaking)*
KEN	*(with a glance at the window)* Poor man.
TREM	*(collecting himself)* Go — to window. What are they doing now?
KEN	*(quickly)* They have gone. I expect they have gone to her room now.
TREM	Are you sure? You're not just saying this to spare me?
KEN	There's nobody in the living-room, Mr Tremayne, cross my heart and hope to die.
TREM	The bedroom? The window on the extreme right.
KEN	Curtains drawn, nothing to be seen.

one's throat, and start counting to ten? And what happens after "ten"? One goes on counting: "Ten plus one, ten plus two . . ." As long as there's the smallest glimmer of hope.

KEN   Can I get you anything? It seems pointless . . .

TREM   Stay where you are! You are not to shift your eyes from the room. What happens afterwards is as important.
One night, after he had gone, she sat and cried. For a long time. Ralph watched her, and she just sat there and cried, till it got dark and Ralph could not see her any more.
That night I wrote her a long letter. I told her everything; about the car crash, my sight, everything.

KEN   You told her that you were having her watched every night?

TREM   Yes, that too. But I never sent off the letter.

KEN   Why not?

TREM   Because I had to dictate the letter to Ralph. Imagine receiving a personal letter like this in someone else's handwriting? With spelling mistakes, and words crossed out?

KEN   Why should Ralph make spelling mistakes?

TREM   Because he is careless, and half-educated.

KEN   *(jumping up)* Mr Tremayne, I'm not going to sit here and have my friend insulted . . .

TREM   *(shouting)* You will sit there, and do as I tell you!
You were hired to do a job, remember?

KEN   *(after a pause, picking up the binoculars)* They have just come out of her room. He's trying to put on his coat. She's pulling it off him again. She seems to be laughing. She's barring the door. He's getting nervous, pointing to his watch. They are having a sort of fight. They're on the settee now. He's got her across his knee, and is starting to spank her. Oh, dear me, what a carry-on!

TREM	*(hoarsely)* You are lying!
KEN	Am I just? Why don't you get someone else from outside to confirm?
TREM	Go on — stop complaining.
KEN	He's taken some of her clothes off again. They seem to be preparing to make love again.
TREM	No! <u>NO</u>!
KEN	Would you rather I drew the curtains, sir? It's hardly decent to watch them, is it now?
TREM	Yes, no — I don't know. *(After a pause)* Watch them. Go on watching them.
KEN	*(primly taking up his binoculars)* It's as I thought, Mr Tremayne: they are making love.
TREM	Describe it.
	There is a long pause
	Describe it, Ken. Describe it!
KEN	Surely you don't expect me to go into anatomical details?
TREM	I expect you to tell me what you see.
KEN	They are on the settee — she is completely naked — I — I don't know . . . it's getting rather dark.
TREM	You don't want to see a man and a woman together, do you? You think it abnormal, don't you? It makes you sick, doesn't it?
KEN	No need to get het up. They're both getting dressed now, anyway. I expect he'll be gone in a minute — what with looking at his watch.
TREM	Where is — she?
KEN	She's got her house-coat — sorry, dressing-gown — on now. She's giving him a kiss now; he's on his way. *(Getting up)*

	Can I have my fruit salad now, please?
TREM	Do what you damn well like.
KEN	Very polite, I'm sure.

KEN *goes off to the kitchen*

TREM	*(exhausted)* Well, and where does that get you? You are alone again, just like me . . .

KEN *enters with a bowl of fruit salad*

KEN	Is there anything further you'll be requiring, sir?
TREM	I must thank you — and apologize.
KEN	*(sitting in the small chair)* No need to do that. You hired me; I did what you wanted, that's all. *(He eats)*
TREM	I completely forgot to settle . . .
KEN	Don't you worry about that! Ralph said you'd see me all right.
TREM	Yes, I'll see you all right . . .

Pause

KEN	It's amazing how long it stays light . . .
TREM	*(excited again)* It's still light? Why didn't you say so, you fool?
KEN	*(rising and putting the bowl on the table)* Don't say you want me to go back! You're not expecting any more fireworks from your little friend tonight?
TREM	Don't try to comprehend other people's thoughts and actions. *(Pointing to the window)* If you please.
KEN	*(resuming his seat in the armchair with bad grace)* Of course, I'm only the hired help — I don't understand nothing. I don't.
TREM	What do you see now?

KEN	There's no one in the dining-room, but there seems to be someone in the kitchen. Maybe she's washing up.
TREM	She never washes up in the evening; she always leaves it till the morning.
KEN	*(maliciously)* Yes, I can believe that, having seen her, got to know her — as one might say — quite intimately.
TREM	You're trying to provoke me, aren't you?
KEN	Me provoke you? Dear me, what gives you that idea, Mr. Tremayne?
TREM	Because you hate me for loving a woman.
KEN	Oh, we're on that again! Quite a pet subject. *(Holding the binoculars to his eyes)* Hold on, here's little Miss Sunshine again, all brisk and cheerful . . .
TREM	What — what is she doing?
KEN	*(secretively)* Aha. No, don't worry, dear, she's only tidying up. Are you expecting another visitor to turn up, then?
TREM	That's the worst of it — that I have to place myself in other people's hands. People like you . . .
KEN	Beggars can't be choosers.
TREM	Describe what you see, while it's still light.
KEN	*(wearily)* She's just busying herself — ordinary household chores.
TREM	Her face? What does she look like? Sad, happy, anxious? Fulfilled?
KEN.	If you want my honest opinion, Mr Tremayne, she looks just — ordinary, as though nothing very special had happened.
TREM	Just a normal sort of evening . . .

KEN	*(triumphantly)* Hold on — not quite as "normal" as you might think, by the look of it!
TREM	What do you mean?
	KEN *gives a low chuckle*
	What are you hinting at? *(Urgently)* Will you kindly tell me what's going on?
KEN	Another visitor, Mr Tremayne. A girl friend, this time . . .
	TREMAYNE, *pale and trembling, gets out of bed*
TREM	Let me see! *(Shouting and groping about)* Let me see! I want to see! *(He knocks over the chair by the bed)*
KEN	*(rising; startled)* Mr Tremayne, careful! You'll do yourself an injury . . .
TREM	*(pressing his face against the window-pane)* I don't believe it, I don't believe it! *(Groaning)* Let it not be true . . .
KEN	*(anxiously)* Mr Tremayne, sir, you must get back to bed . . .
	He takes TREMAYNE's *arm protectively*
TREM	*(completely beside himself)* Is it true? Look — keep looking!
KEN	It's too dark — and they've drawn the curtains now . . .
	Pause
TREM	Are you sure? A woman?
KEN	Positive, sir.
TREM	*(turning his back to the window and beginning to sob)* That was why, Ken. Guide me back to bed . . .
	KEN *helps* TREMAYNE *back to bed.* KEN *turns on the light*
	You understand now, don't you? The pills — on the sideboard there . . .
KEN	*(picking up a box of pills as directed)* I'll get you a glass of water, sir. Just lie quietly.
	KEN *goes off to the kitchen*

TREM	Ken! Ken, are you there? *(Calling)* You haven't left, have you? *(Frightened)* Ken!
	KEN *enters with a glass of water*
KEN	Here's your glass of water. Now — *(reading the label on the box)* — it says here "to be taken two at a time". There we are.
	KEN *gives the pills to* TREMAYNE *and makes sure he drinks the water*
	You'll feel much better soon.
TREM	*(lying back)* Yes, they work wonders. They send me to sleep. *(After a pause)* Ralph will be here in a moment. He will settle with you. He'll see you all right.
KEN	Not to worry. Just relax and go to sleep.
TREM	You can switch the light out, Ken, and — sit and wait in the kitchen. You'll find newspapers . . .
KEN	I'll make myself comfortable, Mr Tremayne.
TREM	*(quietly)* Good night, Ken — and thank you. Maybe another time . . .
KEN	Good night, Mr Tremayne. Happy dreams.
	KEN *switches off the light then goes into the ante-room, closing the bedroom door and giving a sigh of relief. He switches on the ante-room light*
TREM	*(whispering)* My beautiful, my princess. Here, put your head on my shoulder — spread your hair over me — like a blanket of gold . . . *(He falls asleep, breathing regularly)*
	There is a long pause, then three soft buzzes from the front door KEN *runs to open it.* RALPH *enters*
RALPH	I'd completely forgotten that I gave you my keys. I hope he hasn't . . .
KEN	He's fast asleep.
RALPH	Well? Everything all right?

KEN   I've had a time of it, I can tell you.

RALPH   Wait, let me just check up.

> *He tiptoes into the bedroom, goes to the window,
> and slightly opens it. He tidies up one or two
> things and picks up a blanket and replaces it on the
> bed —* KEN *follows* RALPH *into the bedroom*

KEN   *(whispering)* I've had a narrow escape.

RALPH   *(anxiously)* Didn't you remember?

KEN   Oh, I remembered all right.

RALPH   The Rouault print?

KEN   Yes, of course.

RALPH   And Gerald?

KEN   Yes — but you see, I also invented another visitor — a
           woman.

RALPH   *(quickly)* You shouldn't have done that.

KEN   *(after a pause)* Sorry. It was an accident. And he'd been
           beastly. *(He pauses, looking at* TREMAYNE*)* Still, he seems
           quite peaceful now. One would never believe . . . *(He
           walks across to the window)* It's all — quiet now. Just one
           or two lights. I really thought I saw her, you know . . .

RALPH   I see her — every night. Of course, I have one advantage
           over you: I really did see her, months ago, before she
           moved. A pretty little thing, she was . . .

> *Pause*

KEN   *(staring out into the darkness)* I wonder — I'd really be
           curious to know — where she's gone . . .

> RALPH *and* KEN *leave the room quietly and go
> into the kitchen.* TREMAYNE *is sleeping peacefully.
> From far away there is the whistle of a train*

END

Dog Accident
by James Saunders

The first stage performance of *Dog Accident* was on the pavement of
Tyburn Way in front of Marble Arch, London, at lunchtime, the 6th
November 1969, with:
Jim Hiley
Geoff Hoyle

An Inter-Action Production designed and directed by ED Berman

Approximate playing time: 25 minutes

PHOTOGRAPH: DAILY TELEGRAPH

A sudden screeching of brakes; a little yelp

1st Onlooker	Poor little tyke . . . . .
2nd Onlooker	It was the dog's fault.
1st O	What?
2nd O	The dog was to blame. They ought not to allow it. Didn't you see?
1st O	See what?
2nd O	What happened.
1st O	I saw.
2nd O	Ran straight into the road, it did. It wasn't the driver's fault. There was nothing he could do.
1st O	Maybe not . . . . .
2nd O	Well what? What could he do?
1st O	Nothing, I suppose. I don't know.
2nd O	Well I know. Nothing. That's what he could do . . . Come on.
1st O	What?
2nd O	Come on. There's no point in hanging around. It's all over now. Come on.
1st O	In a minute . . . . .
	Pause
2nd O	Come on . . . . .
1st O	There's no hurry.
2nd O	I know there isn't, it isn't a question of hurry . . . . . Are you going to stand here all day looking at a dead dog?
	Pause

Well are you? Are you?

1st O	It isn't dead.
2nd O	What?
1st O	It's not dead.
2nd O	Of course it's dead. Come on.
1st O	I tell you it's not dead . . . . . .
2nd O	How do you know?
1st O	I just know.
2nd O	You just know. How do you know?
1st O	It moved.
2nd O	I didn't see it move.
1st O	Just because you didn't see it move, doesn't mean it didn't move.
2nd O	And just because you say it moved, doesn't mean it did move.
1st O	I tell you I saw it move. It moved its leg.
2nd O	You say it moved its leg.
1st O	I wouldn't say it moved its leg if I didn't see it, would I?
2nd O	You think you saw it. You think so . . . . . Come on. The dog's dead.
1st O	It's not dead.
2nd O	Once and for all —
1st O	Look at it, then. Look at it!
2nd O	What for?

1st O	You'll see it move.
2nd O	It can't move. It's dead. I don't want to look at a dead dog.
1st O	Look at it, just look at it . . . . .
2nd O	It's not moving . . . It's dead.
1st O	There! There! Twice. It moved its leg. Twice. Now. Did you see that?
2nd O	I saw it.
1st O	Well?
2nd O	The dog's dead.
1st O	It moved its leg!
2nd O	I know it moved its leg. I'm not denying it moved its leg. Rigor mortis . . . . .
1st O	What?
2nd O	Rigor mortis.
1st O	What do you mean, rigor mortis?
2nd O	Rigor mortis. Chickens do the same thing.
1st O	Are you trying to tell me —?
2nd O	I tell you chickens do the same. If you cut a chicken's head off it runs around . . . Afterwards.
1st O	With no . . . ?
2nd O	Afterwards
1st O	I don't believe it.
2nd O	I've seen it happen.
1st O	What?

2nd O	I've seen it.
1st O	You've <u>seen</u> a chicken — ?
2nd O	Running around after its head has been cut off. Now that's enough of it . . . Rigor mortis. The dog's dead. Come on.
1st O	It moved again.
2nd O	Rigor mortis. Come on.
1st O	In a minute.
2nd O	Come on. The dog's dead.
1st O	It's not dead . . . . . .
2nd O	What makes you so sure?
1st O	I just know it's not <u>dead</u>!! I just know it's not <u>dead</u>! Do you think I can't tell a live dog from a dead dog?
2nd O	You've never seen a dead dog.
1st O	I've seen live dogs . . .
2nd O	Well, it makes no difference. It's nearly dead.
1st O	Nearly dead is different from dead.
2nd O	There's nothing we can do . . .
1st O	I'm not saying there is anything we can do.
2nd O	Then what are you hanging about for?
1st O	There . . .
2nd O	What?
1st O	Didn't you hear?
2nd O	Hear what?
1st O	It made a noise.

31

2nd O	I didn't hear anything . . . Whined?
1st O	A sort of whine . . .
2nd O	After all, the dog was to blame . . .
1st O	What do you mean, the dog was to blame?
2nd O	It was the dog's fault. It ran into the road.
1st O	I know it did.
2nd O	Then the dog was to blame.
1st O	How can a dog be to blame?
2nd O	The dog ran into the road —
1st O	I know the dog ran into the road. Why shouldn't it run into the road?
2nd O	There's why it shouldn't. There . . . It was the dog's own fault.
1st O	I know it was, I'm not saying it wasnt . . . .
2nd O	Then what are you arguing about?
1st O	But the dog isn't to blame.
2nd O	You think the motorist was to blame?
1st O	I don't know whether he was or not.
2nd O	Then whose fault was it?
1st O	It was the dog's fault.
2nd O	Then the dog was to blame.
1st O	It wasn't to blame!
2nd O	Then who was?

1st O	I don't <u>know</u>, I don't know whether anyone was to blame. I only know the dog wasn't to blame. You can't blame the dog!
2nd O	Why can't you?
1st O	Because he's a dog.
2nd O	He should have had more sense.
1st O	But he didn't.
2nd O	Well, there you are.
1st O	What do you mean, there you are? You can't blame a dog for not having more sense.
2nd O	Why can't you?
1st O	<u>Because</u> he's a <u>dog</u>. A dog's a dog.
2nd O	Can't a dog have more sense than another dog?
1st O	You can't blame a dog for not having more sense than another dog.
2nd O	Why can't you?
1st O	Because there's no stopping it. If you can blame a dog for not having more sense than another dog, you can blame a man for not having more sense than another man. There's no stopping it.
2nd O	We're not talking about men.
1st O	It's the same thing.
2nd O	You mean a dog's the same as a man?
	Pause
	You mean a dog's the same thing as a man?
1st O	An unintelligent dog to an intelligent dog is the same as an unintelligent man to an intelligent man!

2nd O	You're mad.
1st O	You can't blame a dog.
2nd O	All right! Anyway, the dog's dead now. Come on.
1st O	It's not dead . . .
2nd O	It's dead now.
1st O	It's not dead. It made a noise.
2nd O	Whined?
1st O	A sort of whine . . . A sort of . . . whine . . . . .
2nd O	That was before.
1st O	Before what?
2nd O	Before. Before.
1st O	Before what?
2nd O	Before it died.
1st O	What?
2nd O	It's not making any noise now, is it? It's not even moving its leg anymore, is it?
1st O	Well?
2nd O	The dog's dead.
1st O	I don't see why you think . . .
2nd O	Just because it made a noise <u>before</u> doesn't mean it's not dead <u>now</u>.
1st O	And just because it's not making a noise <u>now</u>, doesn't mean it's <u>dead</u> now.
2nd O	Come on.
1st O	There's blood on its neck . . . .

2nd O	I know there's blood on its neck. Do you think I can't see? I don't want to stand here looking at blood on a dog's neck, if you do.
1st O	I don't want to look at blood on its neck.
2nd O	Then what are you looking at it for? What are you looking at it for? Why?
1st O	Someone ought to look at it, ...
2nd O	Why? Why?
1st O	Someone ought to look at it, that's all.
2nd O	Why?
1st O	If you were lying in the road with blood on your neck, wouldn't you want to know that somebody had looked at it? If you were lying with blood on your neck, dying . . . . .
2nd O	I'd want someone to fetch an ambulance.
1st O	If nobody could fetch an ambulance. If there were <u>no</u> ambulances, <u>no</u> bandages, <u>no</u> iodine . . . .
2nd O	But there are.
1st O	But if there weren't . . . . . .
2nd O	What do you want me to say?
1st O	If you were dying with blood on your neck and you knew nobody could help you . . .
2nd O	Well?
1st O	Wouldn't you want to know that <u>somebody</u> had . . . . looked at you?
2nd O	At the blood on my neck?
1st O	Yes.

35

2nd O	Why?
1st O	Wouldn't you?
2nd O	No . . . I'd be ashamed.
1st O	<u>Ashamed</u> . . .
2nd O	Anyway, <u>I'm</u> not a dog.
1st O	It comes to the same thing.
2nd O	You mean a dog's the same as a man?
1st O	It comes to the . . .
2nd O	You mean a dog's the same as —
1st O	It's all suffering, isn't it?
2nd O	Dogs are different.
1st O	You mean dogs don't suffer? Is that what you mean?
2nd O	I don't want to talk about it . . . You're morbid, that's your trouble.
1st O	I'm not morbid —
2nd O	You're morbid. You just chew on things. You get hold of something sad you chew and chew on it. As if there wasn't enough trouble in the world . . .
1st O	I'm not morbid . . . . .
2nd O	You get something in you mind and you won't let it go. <u>A dead dog</u> . . . . .
1st O	The dog's not dead! You're just saying the dog's dead because you don't want to . . . .
2nd O	The dog's dead!
1st O	The dog's not dead!

2nd O	Dead! Dead!
1st O	It's not dead!! It's not dead!! It's not . . . .
2nd O	Come on . . . Well, are you coming? Or not? . . . . Once and for all, are you coming? All right, stay then. Stay as long as you like. Much good may it do the two of you . . . . . . I'm going.
1st O	All right, go, go.
2nd O	Are you coming?
1st O	No.
2nd O	Why not? ·
1st O	You go . . .
2nd O	What are you —?
1st O	I'm waiting for the dog to die . . .
2nd O	You're morbid, I've said all along you're just —
1st O	I'm not morbid . . . . I'm not morbid . . . .
2nd O	You're morbid. You <u>want</u> the dog to be alive. You want it. That's what you're standing here for. You're standing here <u>wanting</u> the dog to be alive. That's what you're doing, isn't it? You're standing here <u>wanting</u> the . . . .
1st O	I don't want the dog to be alive. I want it to be dead. I want it to be dead!
2nd O	You want it to be alive. That's why you're standing here. You're morbid. You're standing here waiting . . . until you can imagine the dog's alive . . . What? What are you doing? Get up: leave it alone and get up. Don't touch it. Do you want to catch something? Leave it alone. What's the matter with you? Haven't you any self respect? Kneeling down to a — look what you're doing. My God look at your hand. How disgusting can you get? Here, wipe it off. For God's sake, wipe it off. Here's my handkerchief. Wipe it off. Come on, we'll go now — and forget about it.

37

1st O	The dog's not dead . . . .
2nd O	You are trying me beyond endurance! . . . Look, I . . . look, I don't understand you, I just don't understand you. What do you want to do? Do you want to spend your life standing here looking at a . . . .? You can't do any good here. It's happening all the time, don't you read the papers? All the time, every day. Not just dogs, Everything. You only have to look at the papers. Burnt,drowned, everything. Crashes, collisions. Only yesterday there was one, fifty people, I read it out to you, you didn't make any fuss about that. Due to be married the next day, she was, everything arranged and then piff . . . Gone, finished, disaster. Every day's the same; disaster, catastrophe, it's too big to imagine, there's too much of it, you can't take it in. Fifty people, sixty people . . . And you stand there looking at one dead dog . . . .
1st O	There goes its leg again . . . .
2nd O	I don't care about its leg. What about those fifty people, what about <u>their</u> legs?
1st O	They're dead.
2nd O	Come on, Come on or we won't get any lunch. Let's go get a Wimpy.
1st O	I don't want a Wimpy.
2nd O	A hot dog then,

1st ONLOOKER looks at him

2nd O	Come on.
1st O	I don't want any lunch.
2nd O	You'll want some when you get there. Look, about four o'clock this afternoon you'll be sitting in the office wishing you'd had that Wimpy. Come and have a Wimpy and forget about the dog. Come on —
1st O	In a minute.
2nd O	You'll feel better if you forget about it.

38

1st O	I know I will.
2nd O	Then come on.
1st O	In a minute.
2nd O	Do you think the dog cares whether you stand here or not?! Do you think the dog even <u>knows?</u>
1st O	I don't know.
2nd O	Well, I do. It doesn't. And if it did know it wouldn't care. Do you think the dog bothers about you?
1st O	It isn't the point whether it bothers about me or not.
2nd O	Then what is the point?
1st O	I want to bother about the dog. <u>That's</u> the point. I want . . . <u>someone</u> to bother about the dog.
2nd O	Why you?
1st O	If I don't nobody else will.
2nd O	Other people have got more sense.
1st O	It isn't a question of sense.
2nd O	Then what is it a question of?
1st O	It's a question of somebody . . . <u>bothering</u> . . . Somebody . . . being here just to . . . to . . .
2nd O	To what, to what?
1st O	To bear witness.
2nd O	Witness?
1st O	(*In a sudden fury*) It's dying! In the road. Dying, and nothing happens!
2nd O	What do you expect to happen when a dog dies?

39

1st O	Nothing
2nd O	What do you expect to happen? Do you want the skies to fall down when a dog dies? Do you want the angels to fly down and bear it up in their wings? Is that what you want, angels?
1st O	I don't want angels.
2nd O	Then what _do_ you want?
1st O	I'm not asking for anything, am I?
2nd O	Then come on.
1st O	In a minute. Just wait a minute. Just till —
2nd O	I don't see the point in it —
1st O	Listen —
2nd O	What?
1st O	Listen . . . .
2nd O	What?
1st O	I thought it made a noise.
2nd O	You're imagining. You've been standing here so long you're imagining.
1st O	Listen . . . There . . .
2nd O	I can't hear anything. You're imagining.
1st O	You must hear it.
2nd O	I tell you it's in your mind.
1st O	In my — ?
2nd O	In your mind. Dead dogs don't make noises. You know what you've got, don't you? You've got a febrile

imagination. You know what that means? Sick. Febrile means sick, you've got a sick imagination. We all know things like this happen. That's enough for most of us. A dog dies, well, well all right, we leave it at that, we forget about it, we've got our lives to live, what's finished is finished. But not for you. You have to get your febrile imagination to work on it, you have to imagine it back to life so you can get a kick out of imagining it dying again. You can't let sleeping dogs lie. It's people like you cause half the trouble in this world. What are you doing?

1st O   Listen . . .

2nd O   Your mind again —

1st O   No. Listen. Listen . . . .

2nd O   Nothing . . .

1st O   <u>Listen.</u>

2nd O   A whine?

1st O   No, not a whine.

2nd O   Then what?

1st O   Its leg again, look . . . Again.

2nd O   Yes, but what noise?

1st O   There, again. And again. Its other leg.

2nd O   What noise, what noise?

1st O   I don't know . . . Why does it shake so?

2nd O   It's dying.

1st O   Not a whine. A sort of . . . A sort of song . . .

2nd O   You're mad.

1st O   Not song. Psalm, a sort of psalm. Like in Sunday school . . . that's it, it was like in Sunday school!

The DOG *screams.*

Pause

The DOG *screams again*

Pause

2nd O	Psalm?
1st O	What?
2nd O	What psalm?
1st O	Psalm?
2nd O	You said —
1st O	I said, I said! Can't you ever stop talking? Can you never, never stop talking! Can't you be silent for a moment, is it out of the question? Do you know so much, that you talk so much? Do you know enough to talk at all?
2nd O	You said —
1st O	It was in my mind, something in my mind. That's all. Let that be an end of it. Something reminded me of something else. Now enough of it . . .
2nd O	The dog's dead . . .
1st O	The dog's dead . . .
2nd O	Like I said all along.
1st O	Yes I could eat a Wimpy.
2nd O	Come on then I'll treat you. Poor little tyke . . . Come on.
1st O	Come on . . . . I'm hungry.

END

Have You Met Our Rabbit?
by Michael Stevens

To
Mike Wedge
who gave me the idea

The first performance of *Have You Met Our Rabbit?* was at the
Ambiance Lunch-Hour Theatre Club at the Oval House, Kennington,
London SE11, on the 21st December 1970, with:
        Prunella Scales
        Robert Coleby

An Inter-Action Production designed and directed by ED Berman

Approximate playing time: 35 minutes

PHOTOGRAPH: INTER-ACTION

*The large main room in the home of a prosperous
European family. A summer's day.*

*It is very hot. At the back of the room the windows
are wide open. The curtains move occasionally in
the breeze. The windows lead out on to a balcony.
A door on one side of the room leads to the stairs,
as this is a first floor flat. On the opposite side
another door leads to the other rooms. There is a
sofa and the usual furniture and a chess board and
pieces.*

*When the curtain rises the door to the stairs is open.
HELLA's voice can be heard on the stairs, shouting.*

HELLA   *(off)*   Erik! Where are you going? *(She pauses)* But he may
come any minute. *(She pauses)* Don't be silly. He may come
at any time.

    The front door slams

Oh . . .

    HELLA enters. She is in her late thirties

It's always Mother. Mother, look over my homework.

    She goes out to the other rooms

(Off)   Mother, will you look after the rabbit? Mother, will
you take me to the rally?

    *She comes back into the room with a pile of
    newspapers*

Mother, will you entertain my friends? *(She puts the chess
pieces away, moves the sofa round, takes out some dirty
crockery and returns with a trowel. Then she pauses)*
Well, I won't. *(She goes over to the mirror and wipes dust
off it. Then she sticks out her tongue at her reflection)*
So there. Anyway, he's English. I don't like the English.
(She sits down. After a pause) They smell. *(After another
pause, she gets up)* I must clean the rabbit. Erik won't
do it, that's for sure.

    *She goes out on to the balcony. There is a pause,
    then a knock at the door. HELLA comes back into*

the room, clutching a Polish white rabbit by the ears

Good God! He's here! I told Erik he would come. And now he's come. *(She goes over to the door and stops, seeing the rabbit. She makes to go back to the balcony)*

The knock comes again. HELLA *opens the door, then steps back*

Come in!

JOHN enters. He is about eighteen years old, Erik's pen friend. He carries luggage

HELLA   You must be John. I'm sorry, I don't speak a word of English.

JOHN   I'm sorry. I only speak English.

They look blankly at each other

HELLA   I'm sorry, I don't understand.

JOHN   Sorry, not with you. Do you speak English?

HELLA   I do not understand.

JOHN   *(slowly)* Do—you—speak—English?

HELLA   *(loudly)* No understand. No English.

JOHN   *(loudly and slowly)* Do—you—speak—English?

HELLA   *(annoyed)* Oh, for Christ's sake . . . *(She notices the rabbit in her arms, and laughs)*

HELLA *goes out on to the balcony*

JOHN   Bloody hell. She doesn't speak English.

HELLA   *(off)* Now get back into your cage, you lumbering parasite. Get in. Get in! That's it. I'm looking forward to the day we eat you.

JOHN   I hope she's all right.

HELLA comes back into the room

HELLA   *(sweetly)* I was just cleaning his cage when you came.

                 JOHN looks blank

            I don't suppose you understand one word of what I'm saying, do you? *(After a pause; more loudly, with mime, pointing)* I was cleaning out the rabbit. Cleaning—*(chewing like a rabbit)* — the <u>rabbit</u>.

            They both laugh. There is a pause

JOHN   I wonder if this is the right house.

            They both laugh again, more forcedly

HELLA   Do sit down.

            JOHN remains standing. HELLA sits on the sofa

            Do sit down. *(She pats the sofa to indicate what he should do)*

            JOHN looks at her. Slowly he crosses the room. He sits down beside her. HELLA stands up quickly. She laughs nervously

            Would you like a drink? *(After a pause)* Drink? *(She puts an imaginary glass to her mouth and drinks)* Glug-glug.

            Laughter. JOHN nods. HELLA nods. They both nod. Renewed laughter

            This is going to be hard work.

            HELLA goes out to the kitchen. JOHN looks after her

JOHN   I wonder what I'm getting. *(After a pause; more concerned)* I wonder if this is the right flat! *(He takes out his wallet and a letter, then goes into the hall to examine the number on the door)* I'm sure this is 3B.

            HELLA returns, after a quick brush-up, with a cold drink.

            JOHN reappears. HELLA looks suspiciously at him

I was just checking the number. *(He points to the letter and the door)*

HELLA *hands him the drink. He takes it*

Thank you.

HELLA   My son is out. *(Slowly)* My—son—Erik

JOHN *recognizes the word and nods*

—*(pointing)*—is out—*(miming)*—swimming. Back soon. *(She points to her watch and demonstrates the movement with her fingers)* Twenty minutes. *(She shows twenty fingers)* Twenty minutes—*(aloud, but more to herself)*—I hope. *(After a pause)* Did you have a good journey? *(She pauses, but finds it impossible to mime)* Are you tired? *(She rests her head on her hands)* Tired?

JOHN   *(smiling and shaking his head)* No.

HELLA   Would you like a wash? *(She mimes washing her face and hands)*

JOHN   *(smiling broadly and shaking his head)* No, thank you.

HELLA   Would you like to eat? *(She goes through voracious eating motions)*

JOHN   *(laughing)* No, thank you.

HELLA   What are you laughing at? *(Raising her voice)* What are you laughing at?

JOHN *stops laughing.* HELLA *stops being annoyed and laughs*

JOHN   God, what's wrong with her? *(He laughs)*

HELLA   What did you say?

JOHN   What was that?

HELLA   Sorry?

JOHN   What?

HELLA	*(very loudly)* <u>I do not understand.</u> *(After a pause)* I'm very sorry. Do forgive me. But it's no use, is it? We don't follow each other. *(At a more normal pace, and almost to herself)* I don't understand anything you say, and I might be speaking — ancient Arabic, for all you know.
JOHN	That was a mouthful.
HELLA	*(with a final attempt)* But my son Erik is — *(pointing)* — out — *(miming)* — swimming. He went out five — *(holding up five fingers)* — minutes before you —*(pointing)* — came. He — *(pointing)* — shouldn't have gone out because you — *(pointing)* — are his — *(pointing)* — guest, and you've — *(pointing)* — come all the way from England — *(vigorously pointing)* — to stay with us — *(pointing)* — and he's — *(pointing)* — the only one who understands a word of English, and he — *(pointing)* — should be here — *(pointing)* — not swimming — *(miming)*. *(Breathlessly)* Shouldn't he?
JOHN	Around the rugged rock the ragged rascal ran. Richard of York Gave Battle In Vain. To be or not to be that is the question, whether 'tis nobler in the mind to suffer — English "A" level.
HELLA	I've no idea what you're saying. It's quite futile for us to go on like this. What's the point?
JOHN	I'm sorry — it doesn't make sense to me. I think we'd better wait until Erik comes back, then we shall be able to understand what we're saying, if you see what I mean?
HELLA	You see, I've only understood one word in all that, and that was Erik. We may just as well be dumb.
JOHN	I think it might be a good idea if we just jacked it in a bit.
HELLA	We aren't getting anywhere.
JOHN	Let's pack.
HELLA	Pointless.
JOHN	Yes.
HELLA	Yes.

There is a long pause. JOHN finds his way to the sofa. HELLA puts a cloth on the table. She offers JOHN a magazine. No words are exchanged. JOHN briefly skims through the magazine. HELLA finds herself a cigarette but does not offer JOHN one.

You smell.

JOHN   *(looking up)* Sorry?

HELLA   You smell. All Englishmen smell. They smell of money. And holiness. *(She comes over and deliberately drops the box of matches near him)*

         JOHN *looks up, and at the matches*

(Nicely) Pick it up. You bastard.

         JOHN *picks up the box and hands it to her. She smiles. He smiles. She takes the box*

Thank you. *(Briskly)* Will you come and help me clean out the rabbit? *(She beckons him over to the balcony)*

JOHN   What is it?

         HELLA *points out, to the balcony*

I can't see anything.

HELLA   I want you to do this job for me, Englishman. It's a dirty job. I insist you do it.

JOHN   Is this where I sleep?

HELLA   The rabbit. *(She makes chewing motions)*

JOHN   We're not eating out here, are we? It'll be a bit cramped.

         HELLA *hands* JOHN *the trowel*

Good Lord, what's for dinner?

HELLA   Clean out the rabbit. Get your hands covered in the muck in his hutch.

49   JOHN   Oh, you want me to clean out the rabbit?

HELLA   The rabbit.

JOHN   Oh, I'm with you. *(His face falls)* What a job.

          HELLA *takes off* JOHN's *jacket. At first he is*
          surprised. Then he realizes what she is doing.

HELLA   You will do better with this off.

JOHN   I've sung for my supper before, but this is the first time
          I've ever had to handle rabbit — muck —

          JOHN *goes out on the balcony*

HELLA   Why should I do all the work?

          JOHN *reappears*

JOHN   — if you'll excuse the expression.

HELLA   The Workers' Committee.

JOHN   Though I suppose it's all the same to you.

          JOHN *goes back on to the balcony*

HELLA   As usual.

          JOHN *reappears*

JOHN   I suppose — I suppose I could even have said —

HELLA   I ordered a carpet —

JOHN   — rabbit turds.

          He coyly skips back on to the balcony

HELLA   — without asking the permission of the Workers'
          Committee. They object to that kind of unilateral action.

          JOHN *reappears*

JOHN   *(in a posh voice)* Rabbit pellets.

HELLA   Everything must be agreed between us.

JOHN   I can't think of anything more vulgar — at least, I can.

50

HELLA   The holy Committee.

                JOHN *goes on to the balcony, mouthing "Shit"*

        It was only a small carpet. A rug, really. For the office.

JOHN   *(off, singing the words)* I think you are an ugly old cow.

HELLA   So I lost my job.

                JOHN *reappears*

JOHN   I love you.

HELLA   What was that you said?

JOHN   Christ!

        He rushes on to the balcony. HELLA *follows him*

HELLA   *(off)* Look what you've done! You made a mess all over
        the balcony. Why couldn't you have been more careful? I
        shall have to clean it up, you know. I suppose.

        HELLA *bustles back in, followed by* JOHN *looking
        more dejected*

        (More restrained) I should have done it myself. *(Looking at
        him)* I suppose you'll want to wash now. *(She starts to take
        the cuff-links out of his shirt)* Keep still a minute. *(She rolls
        his sleeves above the elbow, and pushes him off to the
        kitchen)*

        JOHN *exits to the kitchen*

        Erik knows the answers. Of course, he is very keen on
        politics. Very keen. Are you keen on politics? He will
        demand an argument with you when he arrives. I would
        like to see you argue with him, Englishman. He will be
        spending some time in the army. I think the army is very
        good for a boy. It makes a boy into a man, his back straight.
        Do you go into the army, Englishman?

        JOHN *comes back in. They look at each other*

JOHN   I do not understand.

        There is a pause. HELLA *becomes more business-*

like. She picks up a tray and goes out for crockery, taking the empty glass with her. JOHN sits on the sofa and puts his feet on it

HELLA returns with crockery and lays the table. She motions to him to take his shoes off. He does so. He rests his head on a cushion. HELLA goes out to prepare the dinner

The sunlight goes

HELLA   *(off in the kitchen; singing)*
The hay is tall
The sun is high
But the scythe hangs rusting in the barn,
For my master dies
Here in the hall.

> *HELLA returns. JOHN is asleep. Eventually she comes over to the sofa to turn on the lamps by a switch below the kitchen door*

Oh. I'd forgotten! You're tired.*(She loosens his tie)* You have been travelling. *(Still loosening the tie, she undoes the top button of his shirt. She removes his tie. After a pause, she undoes two more buttons, and turns back his shirt. There is a pause. She looks at him. She remembers. She gets up and turns away)* I would like you. *(She turns. More loudly)* I would like you!

> *JOHN wakes. As she speaks he buttons up his shirt*

Englishman, lie with me. Lie with me, John. It is strange that I can talk to you like this, that I can say to you what I feel and want. *(She sits near him)* Strange to say that I would like to touch you, even now as you sit there buttoning up the shirt which I undid, because I wanted to see you, to see under the shirt. *(After a pause)* I don't think I could ever say that to anyone else, John.

> *JOHN ties his tie. He realizes*

JOHN   You! You took off my tie, didn't you? Didn't you?·And I suppose it was you who . . . Christ! You're probably a raving sexual maniac! Did you undo my shirt? Some place, this is! Aren't you going a bit far? I mean, I don't normally

have my clothes whipped off me while I'm asleep, you
know. Particularly in a strange house, by a middle-aged —
randy — female.
Christ! I hope that's all you did, you . . .

HELLA   You seem a little more energetic now, John.

JOHN   Do you do this often?

HELLA   And embarrassed.

JOHN   You randy old . . .

HELLA   Take your shirt off, John

JOHN   Some holiday this is going to be.

HELLA   Just to please me.

JOHN   I hadn't been in the room five minutes —

HELLA   Or would you rather have dinner?

JOHN   — before you — whatever you did. And I'm here for a month!

HELLA   It's rabbit for dinner. *(She laughs)*

> There is a pause. JOHN *moves round the room,*
> *restless*

         Lie down again, Englishman, lie down.

JOHN   Listen.

HELLA   Lie down.

JOHN   Please.

HELLA   You look better lying down.

JOHN   Listen.

HELLA   *(laughing)* What's the matter?

JOHN   Don't laugh. Listen.

HELLA	Sit down, John, sit down.
JOHN	Will you listen?
HELLA	Please yourself. *(She smiles)*

> JOHN *takes off his tie and undoes the top button.*
> HELLA *stops smiling*

Take your time.

JOHN	I thought that'd make you sit up. *(He moves slightly, recollecting)* You don't mind if I talk to you, do you? I know you can't answer that, but I ask out of habit. I talk out of habit, too, I suppose. It seems ridiculous for two human beings to sit together and not talk, doesn't it?
HELLA	I wonder if you like red cabbage.
JOHN	Coming along in the train, I looked out and I thought, "This is a beautiful country." There was an old man opposite me. He looked very old. I'm terrified of being old. Silly, isn't it? To be young and to be afraid of being old. But to be like that man. He couldn't walk — he shuffled from his seat and his eyes didn't see beyond the glass of the window. His head, moving, nodding all the time. His skin wrinkled. Think. I shall be like that. I want to stay as I am. Of course, I tell people my plans. University. I want to study. And I looked out of the window. The country never gets old, does it? It seems — oh, I don't know — it seems to be young always. I want to be young always.
HELLA	Because it's red cabbage for dinner.
JOHN	I wanted to speak to him. The old man, I mean. But I didn't know any of the words. Like you. I don't know how to talk to you. I felt young again, not knowing the words, like a child. But not happy like a child. More of a dream. I wanted the words to speak. And there were none.
HELLA	I wonder where Erik is. Dinner'll be ready soon.
JOHN	It's all right for you. I've been silent, really, for hours. I want to talk to you. I'm talking now, I suppose, but you're

not listening. You're watching my mouth go up and down, and you can hear the sounds come out, but you're not listening to me. It makes me feel dead. I would like to talk to you. Properly. I wish you could hear me. Well, I know you can hear me, but I mean understand me. I shall have to get Erik to teach me some words. Still, you <u>are</u> listening.

HELLA   *(after a pause)* You spoke gently to me then.

JOHN   Perhaps we shall get on better when Erik comes.

HELLA   I didn't understand you, but you spoke gently.

JOHN   All the same . . .

HELLA   I had forgotten how gently men could speak. *(She goes up to him and takes his hands. After a pause; loudly)* And you're staying for a month.

> *She releases his hands. They begin to talk simul-*
> *taneously, talking more and more loudly in a*
> *pleasant attempt to shout each other down*

JOHN   I'm glad you did that. Don't say anything more for a bit. Just don't say anything. Well, if you're going to talk, remember I can talk as loud as you. *speaking* I can <u>shout</u> . . . *(He shouts)* *together*

HELLA   He's staying for a month. A whole month. Think of that, Hella. Now listen to him. Listen to him. If you raise your voice I shall raise mine. I shall <u>scream</u> . . . *(She screams)*

> *They both shout and scream until they run out of*
> *breath. Then they stop, exhausted. They laugh.*
> *They both flop about, recovering their breath.*
> *JOHN's shirt sleeves flap. Seeing them, HELLA goes*
> *to the table for his cuff-links. She tries to put them*
> *into his shirt sleeves. JOHN whirls and circles away*
> *from her. She runs round him. They laugh again.*
> *They pick up momentum. Noise now, and*
> *movement. JOHN spins like a top, crashing into a*
> *table. He hits her accidentally. She recoils. He*
> *moves to her, sorry. She is pretending. She throws*
> *a cushion at him. It misses and sails out of the*
> *window. Laughter. They pause. Suddenly there is*
> *the sound of the front door opening and closing.*
> *Panic*

55

HELLA   Good Lord! It's Erik! Quick — the rabbit, where is it?

She rushes off on to the balcony

JOHN *makes himself presentable*

HELLA *reappears with the cushion*

It's all right. *(She rushes over to the door, opens it, and shouts)* Erik! Is that you? John's come! *(To JOHN)* Look at your tie. It's round your neck. *(She smiles, goes over to him, and straightens his tie)* I'm so glad you've come.

END

Companion Piece
by Michael Stevens

This play is dedicated
to
the Fourth Year Leavers.
for what they taught me
Wolverhampton 1978

The first performance of *Companion Piece* was at The Ambiance
Lunch-Hour Theatre Club at The Almost Free Theatre, London W1,
on the 8th December 1971, with:
 Corin Redgrave
 Simon Rouse

An Inter-Action Production designed by Gabriella Falk and
directed by ED Berman

Approximate playing time: 30 minutes

PHOTOGRAPH: INTER-ACTION

*The acting area represents a river bank. Two paths
lead away, one to the road, one to a wood. The
river is in the audience.
A fifteen-year-old* BOY *is seen setting up his fishing
tackle. He is surrounded by a basket, keep-net,
maggots, folding seat, rod etc. A bicycle lies on its
side.
After a while a* MAN *enters pushing a bike, more
antique than the* BOY's.
The BOY *sees him.*

MAN   Hello.

BOY   Oh. Hello.

         The man pushes his bike into the centre and rests it

MAN   Where are the others?

BOY   Coming in a bit.

MAN   Good.

         The man puts his tackle down

     Have you started yet?

BOY   No.

MAN   Good spot?

BOY   Alright, yes.

         *The man continues to assemble his kit. Both spend
some time on this
Pause in speech*

MAN   Had you been here long?

BOY   You mean when you came?

MAN   Yes.

BOY   No.

         Pause

MAN	What time are the others coming?
BOY	They'll be here in a bit.
	Pause
	Taylor's got a job Saturday mornings.
MAN	Oh. Where does he work?
BOY	Cope's.
MAN	What does he do?
BOY	Delivery.
MAN	Oh.
	Pause
	What about Maine?
BOY	I dunno where he is.
	BOY *gets up*
MAN	Where 's the best place?
BOY	About here. I'll just go and get a prop.
	BOY *moves towards the wood*
MAN	(*calling*) Cooke!
COOKE	Sir?
MAN	Get me one while you're at it, will you?
	COOKE *goes.* MAN *completes his job. Eventually* COOKE *returns with two props*
	Thanks.
COOKE	What kind of bait are you using? (*They compare*)
MAN	How do you get maggots that colour?

COOKE   You feed them this stuff. You can turn them all colours, pink, blue, yellow. (*slight pause*) It doesn't hurt them.

They prepare to cast and begin. Pause

MAN   Tell me, what's your first name, Cooke? I can't go on calling you Cooke here. Your initial's . .

COOKE   T.

MAN   T. But the others call you . . .

COOKE   Cosher.

MAN   Yes, Cosher. Why's that?

COOKE   It just happened.

MAN   It seems strange. Of course Farmer's nickname is 'Taxi' which doesn't make sense. He's not that fast. And Layton's name is 'Haggis', but he isn't Scottish, as far as I can make out.

COOKE   Layton? Scotch? He came here from Luton.

MAN   What do they call you at home?

COOKE   You name it!

MAN smiles. Pause

Tim.

MAN   Right.

The rods are settled on their props and both sit. Pause

You don't have a job on Saturdays, then, Tim? Like the others

TIM   No. I just do the papers. It's enough.

MAN   How much do you get?

TIM   Quid a week.

MAN	Suppose you get up early?
TIM	Half past six.
MAN	Evenings as well?
TIM	Yes.

Long pause. MAN *slumps.* TIM *remains. It grows warm. Fly hovers.* MAN *brushes it off. Fly returns, settles.* MAN *brushes it away. Fly persists*

MAN	(*deliberately but not too loudly*) Bugger off!

There is no reaction. TIM *continues to stare at the water.* MAN *looks at* TIM. TIM *continues to stare.* MAN *settles down again. Pause*

TIM	I didn't know you swore, sir.
MAN	I don't usually. (*Looks at* TIM) I mean, I <u>do</u> usually. I don't swear at school. (*pause*) At least I <u>do</u> swear at school. In the Staff Room. Sometimes. I don't swear in class.
TIM	We swear in the yard.
MAN	Yes.
TIM	Everybody swears.
MAN	Yes.
TIM	Sir?
MAN	Must you keep on calling me sir?
TIM	Sorry.

Pause

MAN	Sorry, you were saying . . .
TIM	I . . . I can't remember what it was.
MAN	Everybody swears.

TIM	Yes. Does old . . . Does Miss Haworth swear?
MAN	Like a trooper.
TIM	(*incredulous*) Does she?
MAN	What do you think?

They exchange glances, turn away and smile

TIM	You know . . .
MAN	Yes.
TIM	It's funny, isn't it?
MAN	What?
TIM	What we said
MAN	What we said?
TIM	About swearing and all that.
MAN	How d'you mean?
TIM	We swear in the Yard
MAN	Yes
TIM	You swear in the Staff Room
MAN	Ye . . es.
TIM	But we don't swear at each other.
MAN	Oh, I don't know.
TIM	Oh you mean when Maine told Farmer to go and . . . .
MAN	Yes.
TIM	Yes.

Pause

Sir?

MAN   Yes.

TIM   If I don't call you 'sir', what can I call you?

MAN   You could call me . . .

TIM   ....

          TIM *uses a nickname. It should refer to some*
          physical feature of the actor playing the part of the
          MAN — *his nose, ears etc.*

MAN   Yes. You could call me ....(*repeating the*
          name). Or . . .

TIM   Or, I could call you Mr Cross.

MR CROSS (*settling for this*) Yes. You could call me Mr Cross.

TIM   Or . . . . .

MR CROSS Or?

TIM   Or I could call you Andrew.
          Pause
          Your name's Andrew, isn't it?

MR CROSS Yes.

TIM   I've heard you talking to Miss Aubrey. (*with a smile*)

MR CROSS Oh?

TIM   Do you mind if I call you Andrew?

MR CROSS Well . . . .

TIM   It is out of school, isn't it, ... sir?

MR CROSS Yes.

TIM   Shall I call you Andrew, then?

MR CROSS   Alright.

Pause

TIM   Well, Andrew, you're sitting on my bloody sandwiches.

ANDREW   (*getting up quickly*) Am I? Sorry. (*They retrieve the sandwiches*) Are they alright?

TIM   Yes. You weren't really sitting on them. D'you want one?

ANDREW   No thanks. (TIM *starts a sandwich*)

TIM   The girls. You call the girls by their Christian names, don't you? Angela and Susan and Carol.

ANDREW   (*with a smile*) And Annie!

TIM   (*recognising the reference, whatever it is*) And Annie! But you call the boys Farmer and Layton and Taylor and Cooke. Why's that then?

ANDREW   Habit I suppose. No. It must go back to the very old schools.

TIM   Yes.

ANDREW   I don't like it very much.

TIM   But you still call me Cooke.

ANDREW   At school, yes.

TIM   And I call you 'Sir' at school. Why don't I call you 'Andrew'?

ANDREW   Well, you don't call your father, 'Fred' do you?

TIM   No.

ANDREW   Well then.

TIM   His name's Harry.

ANDREW   I asked for that.

64

TIM	But I don't call him 'Sir', either, do I?
ANDREW	What do you call him?
TIM	I don't call him 'Sir'.
ANDREW	I don't want to be called 'Sir'.
TIM	But we do! Why don't I call you 'Andrew'?
ANDREW	At school?
TIM	At school.
ANDREW	It's too personal.
TIM	Oh.
ANDREW	In school.

Pause

TIM	Andrew?
ANDREW	Yes.
TIM	How much do <u>you</u> get?
ANDREW	How much what?
TIM	How much do you get a week?
ANDREW	You mean money?
TIM	I told <u>you</u>. I get £1 a week for papers. How much do you get? It's out of school.
ANDREW	Yes, I know, but . . it's a personal question.
TIM	It's alright for you.
ANDREW	What do you mean?
TIM	You can say what <u>you</u> want

ANDREW   How?

TIM   You ask all the personal questions.

ANDREW   I asked you how much a week you get paid for delivering papers, that's all. It's not a personal question.

TIM   What is it then?

ANDREW   It's not the same.

          Pause

ANDREW   It was just a way of starting the conversation I suppose.

TIM   Oh.

          Pause

ANDREW   If I don't ask questions, you won't say anything.

          Pause

          Will you?

TIM   It's just like being in class again, that's all.

ANDREW   I see.

TIM   Have you got a job, Cooke, and all that.

ANDREW   All right.

TIM   'What time do you get up? What did you have for breakfast?'

          Pause

ANDREW   £19.

          Longer pause. No reaction

TIM   It's too warm. I think we've had it.

ANDREW   You're sulking.

TIM   Teachers — they're all alike. Boss of the show. Always the same. Why can't you be normal?

TIM *begins to pack up his kit.* ANDREW *realises
he's unable to halt events*

ANDREW   I'll give you a hand.

TIM   It's alright. (*They work together*)

ANDREW   Don't forget these weights.

TIM   Thanks.

ANDREW   Net.

TIM   Right.

ANDREW   O.K.?

TIM   Yes.

                    Pause

ANDREW   Sorry you're going.

TIM   It's too warm.

ANDREW   I think I'll stay.

         TIM *picks up his bike and prepares to push it off*
         Goodbye.

TIM   Cheers.

ANDREW   See you on Monday.

TIM   Yes. First period.

ANDREW   Don't be late.

TIM   (*wheeling his bike*) Right.

ANDREW   What shall I say if the others come?

TIM   What others?

ANDREW   Maine . . and Taylor.

TIM	They've got jobs, haven't they?
ANDREW	Yes I didn't know that. I expect they'll come this afternoon
TIM	You're welcome.
ANDREW	(*gently*) Bugger off.
	Pause
TIM	Is that all you get a week? £19 a week. Our kid brought home £28 last week.
ANDREW	Thanks for the commercial.
TIM	Any time.
ANDREW	Go on — hop it.
TIM	You mean — 'bugger off'.
ANDREW	Fair enough.
TIM	That's what you say at school.
ANDREW	'Bugger off'?
TIM	'Fair enough'.
ANDREW	Do me a favour.
TIM	Bugger off?
ANDREW	Let's have one of those sandwiches before you go.
TIM	You sat on them.
ANDREW	What are they? Jam?
TIM	Crisps sandwiches.
ANDREW	Crisps sandwiches! Yous must be joking.
TIM	(*diverted*) Hey! Your float!

ANDREW   Hell!

> ANDREW *gets up, and* TIM *rests the bike and comes over. Improvisation*

ANDREW   Nearly, Tim, nearly.

TIM   Caught three roach last week.

ANDREW   Here?

TIM   No. Robley Pool.

ANDREW   Heavy?

TIM   Not above ten ounces.

ANDREW   Oh.

TIM   Are you in love with me?

> *Pause*

ANDREW   You what?

TIM   You know, are you . . ?

ANDREW   Do you think that?

TIM   No, I don't think you are. You're married.

ANDREW   I had heard.

TIM   Besides, I've seen you with Miss Aubrey. (*with a smile*)

ANDREW   You don't miss much.

TIM   It just interests me — why you arranged this trip.

ANDREW   I thought it might help.

TIM   Help?

ANDREW   This is out of school . . .

TIM   You can say that again.

69

ANDREW   It's easier to get on with each other. Out of school. I can talk to my own kids easier than I can talk to you.

TIM   You should see our old man. Gets on your wick. And he's always in the bloody doghouse.

ANDREW   Does she get on at him?

TIM   Who?

ANDREW   Your mother.

TIM   D'you want another sandwich?

ANDREW   Thanks. (*He eats*)

    Pause

    This isn't what I expected.

TIM   I told you they were crisps sandwiches.

ANDREW   I don't mean that, you berk.

TIM   Who are you calling a 'berk', twitface?

ANDREW   You, twitface.

TIM   I shan't give teacher any more sandwiches.

ANDREW   You crafty Arab.

TIM   Right — that's your lot.

ANDREW   I shan't do my homework.

TIM   You haven't done it anyway. You forgot your dinner. How many times have I told you? (*warming to his imitation*) If I've told you once I've told you a thousand times. It's no good coming to my lessons if you're not prepared. I brought my sandwiches. You can't accuse me of forgetting my sandwiches. Where are your sandwiches? Write out fifty times, "I must not forget my sandwiches when I want to chat up little boys". And let me have them first thing in . . .

ANDREW   Jack it in.

TIM   Well, you wanted to chat me up, didn't you?

ANDREW   Give us another sandwich.

TIM   Didn't you?

ANDREW   O.K. O.K. If you want it that way.

TIM   Why does it matter?

                    A long pause while Andrew searches for an answer

ANDREW   Teaching is difficult sometimes.

TIM   You mean like when Farmer gobbed on Angela . . . ?

ANDREW   Not only that.

TIM   Anyway he left at Easter.

ANDREW   We don't really trust each other. You think I'm somebody
          to beat. We think . . . .

TIM   What?

ANDREW   We think you're somebody to beat, too.

TIM   Yes. And sometimes we get beaten!

ANDREW   There is something which is wrong.

TIM   We've finished the sandwiches.

ANDREW   Pity.

TIM   My old man hated school.

ANDREW   It's not that. I have a theory . . . .

TIM   Me?

ANDREW   Tim, you're incorrigible.

TIM   Don't be filthy.

ANDREW   But look who's talking.

TIM   What do you mean?

ANDREW   About chatting you up.

TIM   That's what it looks like to me.

ANDREW   Well, answer me this.

TIM   Go on.

ANDREW   Why aren't Maine and Taylor here?

TIM   What do you mean?

ANDREW   Why aren't Maine and Taylor here?

TIM   I don't know why you asked them in the first place.

ANDREW   You seem to get on with them alright to me.

TIM   Pair of drips.

ANDREW   So — why weren't they here?

TIM   Because they're working.

ANDREW   Because they're working. So . . .

TIM   So?

ANDREW   So you knew they wouldn't be here? So who's chatting who up?

              TIM *gestures. Pause*

TIM   Your tyre's flat.

ANDREW   Hell, is it?

TIM   Might be the valve.

ANDREW   You just let it down?

TIM   Come off it.

ANDREW	I'll pump it up.
TIM	(*as* ANDREW *tries*) Is it staying up?
ANDREW	Yes. I think it'll hold.
TIM	I doubt it.
ANDREW	I'll test it again in a minute.
TIM	No, it's soft already.
ANDREW	Sure?
TIM	Feel.
ANDREW	Blast.
TIM	Got a puncture kit?
ANDREW	Yes.

TIM *lifts the bike upside down*

TIM	I'll do it.
ANDREW	You won't.
TIM	Got any levers?
ANDREW	Sidepocket of the saddlebag.
TIM	(*emptying the pocket and producing a mouth organ*) What's this?
ANDREW	The other side.
TIM	What't this, inside here?
ANDREW	Pass me the levers, in the other pocket.
TIM	Can you play it?
ANDREW	Yes.

TIM	Go on then. I'll get the tube out.
ANDREW	Pass me the levers.
TIM	Here you play this. I'll use the levers.
ANDREW	If you like.
	TIM *removes the tyre and takes out the inner tube while Andrew, a little self-consciously at first, and then more confidently, plays*
ANDREW	You're doing a grand job. I'll let you clean it for me on Monday.
TIM	Get knotted. Anyway I'm in court.
ANDREW	You?
TIM	Didn't you know?
ANDREW	No.
TIM	Don't they crow about it, the teachers?
ANDREW	We don't get to know everything.
TIM	You want a new inner tube.
ANDREW	Could be.
TIM	There's more patches than tube.
ANDREW	How are you going to find the hole?
TIM	I'll manage. I always do.
ANDREW	Water?
TIM	I'll find it. It's alright. It must be pretty big.
ANDREW	Are you really in court on Monday?
TIM	Don't pump me.
ANDREW	Sorry I spoke.

TIM	It's my affair.
ANDREW	Then why mention it?
TIM	Who the hell are you to tell me what to do?
ANDREW	You want me to listen to you or not?
TIM	You're not teacher, now, you know.
ANDREW	I think I am.

Pause

TIM	That's your trouble. Always playing teacher.
ANDREW	What's biting you?
TIM	Telling me what to do.
ANDREW	You're doing it yourself.
TIM	What.
ANDREW	Telling me what to do.
TIM	Mend your own bike.
ANDREW	No. You do it. You wanted to.
TIM	Well, let me do it then.
ANDREW	Right.

Pause

TIM	Found it.
ANDREW	Good.
TIM	Won't be long now.
ANDREW	I had a puncture once in Ireland. Did I ever tell you about it?
TIM	No.

ANDREW   Outside a monastery.

TIM   Monastery.

ANDREW   We were on holiday. Cycling from Cork. There's plenty of
          monasteries in Ireland. And I had this puncture. Just
          outside the gates. It was getting dark, too. Do you want
          the patches?

TIM   Pass them over.

ANDREW   This?

TIM   Is there a bigger one?

ANDREW   (*passing one*) Anyway, we stayed the night in this
          monastery. They didn't charge either.

TIM   For nothing?

ANDREW   Well, they ask you to put something towards the place. I
          can't remember the buildings much. Or the men. But I
          remember the stillness. The stillness. Away from the road,
          and the town. You walked in the garden and it was as if
          there was nowhere else. There was darkness. And the
          garden. And nowhere else. They'd mended my puncture,
          too, in the morning. We cycled off. And I shall remember
          the stillness and the garden, as if it . . . as if it was
          happening to someone else.

TIM   I know.

                   Pause

          It's done.

ANDREW   Thanks.

TIM   Just let it dry.

ANDREW   Very good of you.

TIM   That's alright.

                   Pause

          It's dry now.

ANDREW   I'll fix it up.

TIM   I'll do it.

ANDREW   No. It's alright.

Pause

MR CROSS   Thanks.

COOKE   Forget it.

MR CROSS   We must go fishing next time.

COOKE   Yes.

Pause

MR CROSS   You off now?

COOKE   Yes.

MR CROSS   (*already forgetting*) See you on Monday.

COOKE   First period.

MR CROSS   Don't be late.

Pause

BOY   See you.

MAN   Cheers.

BOY goes. MAN remains. He plays the tune again, then stares into the water. Lights fade.

END

Dogg's Our Pet
by Tom Stoppard

The first performance of *Dogg's Our Pet* was at The Ambiance Lunch-Hour Theatre Club at The Almost Free Theatre, London W1, on the 8th December 1971, with:

> Geoff Hoyle
> Bob Hescott
> Patrick Barlow
> Jim Hiley
> Katya Benjamin
> Charles Hubbard

An Inter-Action Production designed by Gabriella Falk and directed by ED Berman

Approximate playing time: 25 minutes

PHOTOGRAPH: INTER-ACTION

"Dogg's Our Pet" is an Opening Ceremony because it was written for the opening of the Almost Free Theatre in Rupert Street, Soho, London, and as such it was first performed on 7th December 1971.

The title is an anagram for Dogg's Troupe, a group of actors operating under the umbrella of Inter-Action whose guiding spirit is Ed Berman, sometimes known as Professor Dogg. The play, or ceremony, was written for the Troupe.

In·rehearsal the play profited a great deal from the invention of the Dogg's Troupe, and the printed text is as much a description of an event collectively arrived at as an author's script; this is a debt which I would now like to acknowledge with gratitude.

T.S.

PREFACE

The linguistic joke behind "Dogg's Our Pet" becomes clear in
performance but in print it needs a bit of explantion.
Consider the following scene. A man (Charlie) is going to build a
platform using pieces of wood of different shapes and sizes. There is a
pile of such pieces a few yards away and a second man is going to throw
Charlie a piece whenever Charlie calls for one. Charlie starts by calling
"Plank!" and is thrown a long flat piece. This may happen several times.
Then Charlie calls "Slab!" and is thrown a thicker piece of wood. This
also happens a few times. Then Charlie calls "Block!" and is thrown a
shorter piece. Similarly, Charlie's calls for "Brick!" and "Cube!"
produce other pieces which he needs for the platform.

A stranger who did not know the language, coming upon this scene,
would conclude that, probably, the different words described different
shapes and sizes of wood. But this is not the only possible interpretation.

Suppose, for example, the second man knows in advance which pieces
Charlie needs, and in what order. In such a case there would be no need
for Charlie to "name" the pieces he wants, but only to indicate when he
is ready for the next one. So the calls might translate thus:—

> Plank = Here!
> Slab = Ready!
> Block = Next!
> Brick = The thrower's name.
> Cube = Thank-you!

The logic of the scene remains intact: the scene works the same way
whichever of the two "languages" is actually being used (in the case of
the second "language" there is an element of coincidence in that a
change of word is followed by a change of shape, but coincidence is not
illogical).

But—and this is the premise of "Dogg's Our Pet"—the scene works in
exactly the same way even if Charlie is using one language while his
helper (Brick) is using the other. And if life for Charlie and Brick
consisted only of building platforms in this manner there would be no
reason for either of them ever to discover that they were each using a
language which was not understood by the other.

But this happy state of affairs would end when a third person begins to
use the language in a way which is puzzling to either Charlie or Brick;
and in the play it is Charlie who finds himself outnumbered.

March music.

The stage is empty. CHARLIE *walks on carrying a small radio which is playing the music. He is wearing overalls, and is some kind of workman or caretaker. He puts the radio on the ground to one side and switches it off. He positions himself somewhere near the centre of the stage. He spits on his hands, ready to work.*

CHARLIE   Plank!

A plank is thrown from the wings into CHARLIE's *waiting hands.* CHARLIE *places it down, at right angles to the footlights.* CHARLIE *resumes his receiving position.*

Plank!

This time he is thrown a plastic football, to his surprise. BAKER, *a schoolboy, enters from the same direction.* BAKER *hops and skips, dodges about, waiting for* CHARLIE *to throw the ball back, keen for a game, but* CHARLIE *freezes him to a standstill. Then* CHARLIE *tosses the ball to him, and resumes his receiving position.*

Plank!

A plank is thrown to him. He lays it down next to the first.

Plank!

A third plank is thrown. He lays it next to the others. He resumes his receiving position. ABLE, *another schoolboy, enters.*

ABLE   *(to* BAKER, *entering)* Plank!

BAKER *throws* ABLE *the ball.*

BAKER   *(to* ABLE*)* Plank!

ABLE *throws* BAKER *the Ball. And so on, a throwing game, till* CHARLIE *freezes them to a standstill.* ABLE *has the ball.* CHARLIE *resumes his receiving position.*

CHARLIE   Plank!

> *A fourth plank is thrown to him. He lays it down so that he has four planks together, a small platform. He spits in his hands and resumes receiving position.*

       Slab!

> *A slab is thrown to him. It is not as long as a plank, but is heavier, being square in cross-section. He lays it on top of the planks so that it runs the same way as the planks. He resumes receiving position each time he calls.*

       Slab!

> *A second slab is thrown and is placed alongside the first.*

ABLE   *(to* BAKER*)* Slab?

BAKER   *(to* ABLE*)* Slab.

CHARLIE   Slab!

> *The ball passes between the boys, and a third slab is thrown to* CHARLIE. CHARLIE *catches the slab and turns to* ABLE *and* BAKER, *who cease playing. The ball is placed on the ground out of the way.* CHARLIE *motions* ABLE *and* BAKER *to come downstage towards him, so that they stand in line between* CHARLIE *and the wing from which the pieces are being thrown, all facing front.* CHARLIE *places the slab next to the other two. The combined width of three slabs is equal to the width of four planks. The "step" since the slabs are shorter than the planks is upstage.* CHARLIE *resumes receiving position.*

CHARLIE   Block!

> ABLE *and* BAKER *put their hands up into receiving position but the block whizzes past them and is caught by* CHARLIE. CHARLIE *places it crossways on top of the slabs. A block is as long as the width of the three slabs, but the same size in cross-section.* CHARLIE *spits on his hands.*

Block!

> ABLE *and* BAKER *dutifully spit on their hands. The block whizzes by in front of them while they are doing this.* CHARLIE *catches the block and places it next to the first one.*

Block!

> ABLE *and* BAKER *give up, turning upstage as the block whizzes past.* CHARLIE *catches it and places it.* BAKER *picks up the ball, throws it to* ABLE, *and then sees that someone is coming.*

BAKER   (*warningly*) Dogg . . .

CHARLIE   (*simultaneously*) Block!

> CHARLIE *catches the fourth block.* ABLE *throws the ball into the wings, towards the man who is supposedly throwing the wood.* DOGG *enters. He is the Headmaster, in black gown and mortarboard. He carries a number of small flags on sticks, and a box of flowers. The flags and flowers are in the school colours, like the boys' ties and caps—say, red and blue. The schoolboys react as schoolboys do in the presence of a strict head.* CHARLIE *pauses.* DOGG *comes in rapidly efficiently, a busy man. He is handing out flags, beginning with the front row of the audience and ending with* ABLE, *and* CHARLIE. *As he does so, he counts the flags.*

DOGG   Sun, dock, trog, slack, pan, sock, slight, bright, nun, (*to* ABLE) tun, (*to* BAKER) what, (*to* CHARLIE) dunce.

> DOGG *also has a clipboard and pencil. He records "dunce" flags*

CHARLIE   What?

DOGG   (*disagreeing with him*) Dunce.

CHARLIE   What??

DOGG   Dunce!

CHARLIE   What???

DOGG, *irritably, to prove that his count is correct, takes the flag back from* CHARLIE, *and recounts all the flags again, pointing to each one*

DOGG   Sun, dock, trog, slack, pan, sock, slight, bright, nun, tun, what, <u>dunce!</u>

Triumphantly he gives CHARLIE *his flag back on "dunce"*

(*witheringly*) Pax!

DOGG *has a flag left over, which he puts down and he picks up the box of paper flowers*

Block!

CHARLIE *expects another block; he turns. He turns back and* DOGG *places the first flower in* CHARLIE's *buttonhole, on the strap of the overall*

Block!

ABLE *moves forward and receives his flower from* DOGG, *and goes back to his place*

Block!

BAKER *moves forward and receives his flower and moves back*

(*automatically with flower*) Block!

But there is no one else on stage. DOGG *picks up the extra flag, and the box, and leaves*

CHARLIE   (*sarcastically*) Block!

A fifth block is thrown, luckily straight into his hands. He places it next to the others. The combined width of the five blocks is equal to five-sixths of the length of a slab. In other words, six blocks would have put a complete new layer on the platform, but since there are only five, the platform is thus given another step. To make this clear: if you walked from the back of the stage towards the audience, you would step up on the planks, then up on the slabs, and then up on the blocks. There are two more steps to come. CHARLIE *spits on his hands*

Brick!

He is thrown a brick. He catches it and lays it crossways on the blocks. A brick is equal in cross-section to a block, but shorter. A brick is twice as long as it is wide, like two cubes stuck together

Brick!

A second brick is thrown. He does the same

Brick!

A third brick is thrown. He does the same

Brick!

*A fourth brick is thrown. He does the same. The fifth call of "*Brick*" is uttered by DOGG as he re-enters*

DOGG   Brick!

A fifth brick is thrown to CHARLIE, who is surprised by it but manages to catch it. DOGG, carrying the extra flag and a flower, enters rapidly, and ABLE and BAKER respond to his call for "Brick" by pointing into the wings where the unseen thrower stands. DOGG goes off towards him, and returns immediately without the flag and flower. He goes out.

CHARLIE regards all this with puzzlement and suspicion. He places the fifth brick and resumes the receiving position

CHARLIE   Brick!

A cube is thrown. But CHARLIE needs a brick to complete the next level of the platform

<u>Brick!</u>

He receives another cube. He sees that two cubes are equal to a brick, so he uses them as the sixth brick. The platform now has four steps.

BAKER and ABLE have been immobilised into a formal position with their flags in their hands. But now, since DOGG seems safely out of the way,

> BAKER *breaks ranks and addresses the unseen thrower*

BAKER   Brick! . . . Plank!

> *The ball is thrown to him*

Cube!

ABLE   (*to* BAKER) Plank! (*he gets the ball*) Cube!

CHARLIE   (*exasperated*) Plank??!

> *The ball is thrown to him. He catches it.* BAKER *sees someone coming*

BAKER   (*warningly*) Dogg . . .

> DOGG *enters, walks straight to* CHARLIE, *who is holding the ball, and confiscates it. He positions* CHARLIE *near the wing, then* BAKER *next to* CHARLIE *and* ABLE *next to* BAKER, ABLE *being nearest the platform and* CHARLIE *nearest the unseen thrower.* DOGG *says to the unseen thrower:*

DOGG   Cube . . .

> *A cube arrives, into* CHARLIE's *hands.* CHARLIE *passes it down the line.* ABLE *places it on the bricks.* DOGG, *satisfied, leaves with the ball.* CHARLIE *spits in his hands and turns to the wings.* ABLE *and* BAKER *copy him*

CHARLIE   Cube!

> *A cube is thrown.* CHARLIE *catches it. Without turning he passes it over his head to* BAKER *who murmurs "Cube" to* CHARLIE, *and passes it over his head to* ABLE, *who murmurs "Cube" to* BAKER *and places it on top of the previous cube.* CHARLIE *completes the sequence by shouting "Cube!" into the wings, and the whole cycle is repeated. It is repeated seven times, very rapidly. The eighth time:*

Cube!

> *He is thrown a slab. He puts it aside impatiently, upstage, and tries again*

Cube!

> *Another slab is thrown. He places this aside*

Cube!!

> *A third slab is thrown. He leans on it in exasperation, and then notices that ABLE, instead of placing the cubes neatly has made a tottering tower out of them. CHARLIE puts aside the third slab, and repositions the boys so that he himself is nearest the platform. He replaces the cubes neatly. There are now eight of them, and one more is needed to finish off the top of the platform. The nine cubes together do not cover the bricks completely; there is a step down*

(*to* ABLE) Cube!

BAKER   (*turning back to* ABLE) Slab?

ABLE   (*to* BAKER) Slab.

CHARLIE   (*correcting*) Cube!

BAKER   (*to wings*) Cube!

> *A block is thrown to him. BAKER is quite unconcerned by this. He passes it to ABLE, who murmurs "Cube" and passes it on to CHARLIE, who accepts it but insists again, "Cube."*

> BAKER *calls into the wings, "Cube!" and the whole movement is repeated twice. Finding himself with three blocks,* CHARLIE *is furious.* BAKER *calls again, "Cube!" and is thrown a block. Immediately* CHARLIE *shouts "Cube!" and another (fifth) block is thrown at* BAKER *who just manages to grasp it though he is still holding the previous one*

BAKER   (*remonstrating with the thrower*) Brick!

> BAKER *dumps his two blocks on* ABLE, *and marches off towards* BRICK, *the thrower.* ABLE

dumps the two blocks on top of the three already held by CHARLIE. CHARLIE *is almost invisible behind the five blocks. In the wings there is a confused altercation between* BAKER *and* BRICK *(. . . Slagbox trinket prank cabrank frankly duderanch bedsock . . .) The words are not heard clearly.* ABLE *looks out interestedly into the wings.* CHARLIE *manages to get* ABLE's *attention.* ABLE *comes to his aid by taking the bottom block of the five held by* CHARLIE. ABLE *looks round for somewhere intelligent to put it, and puts it on top of the other four blocks, so* CHARLIE *is back where he started, carrying five. One way or another,* CHARLIE *manages to get himself out from under the five blocks without damage. He abandons the job, picks up his radio and turns it on.*

The radio emits the familiar pips, and then a voice, says, "Check mumble hardly out" *in a particular inflection consistent with an announcer saying "Here are the football results." And it becomes quickly apparent that this is what the radio is giving out, in spite of the language used, the inflections, that is the speech rhythms, are clearly following the familiar cadences associated with home wins, away wins and draws. Here is a translation of the numbers:—*

Nil = quite
1 = sun
2 = dock
3 = trog
4 = slack
5 = pan

In addition, "Clock" and "Foglamp" correspond to "City" and "United."

Thus, the result, "Haddock Clock quite, Haddock Foglamp trog" would be delivered with the inflections appropriate to, say, "Manchester City nil, Manchester United 3" — an away win. The radio starts by saying, "Oblong Sun" with the inflection of "Division One."

RADIO   Dogtrot quite, Flange dock; Cabrank dock, Blanket Clock quite; Tube Clock dock, Handbag dock; Haddock Clock quite, Haddock Foglamp trog; Wonder quite, Picknicking pan . . .

> ABLE *whistles at that — a five-nil away win.*
> CHARLIE *has begun by taking out his football pool coupon at the beginning of the announcements, and from another pocket a stub of pencil. As the radio proceeds, CHARLIE examines his coupon minutely, turns it over, looks at it upside down, and finally screws it up and throws it away*

. . . Stupid Clock slack, Hog sun; Slick Foglamp sun, Hag Foglamp dock . . .

> CHARLIE *turns the radio off.* BAKER *enters carrying a sixth block*

BAKER (*warningly*) Dogg . . .

> CHARLIE *goes to the receiving position and angrily shouts into the wings*

CHARLIE Brick! Slab! Plank! Block!

> *A cube is thrown to him*

(*thankfully*) Cube!

> CHARLIE *puts the cube in place, which completes the platform.* DOGG *enters with a long piece of ribbon rolled up. He pins or hooks the ribbon on one side of the stage, as high as he can reach, and unrolls it across the stage, similarly fixing the other end. There is now a ribbon, in school colours, stretched across just in front of, and a few feet higher than, the platform*

> CHARLIE *watches DOGG do this.* BAKER *and* ABLE *meanwhile reassemble the spare blocks and slabs into a wall. There are three slabs and six blocks. These nine pieces have been scrawled on all sides with indecipherable signs. When the wall is completed, these signs spill into each other over the cracks in the wall, and can now be seen to read:—*

> *DOGG*
> *POUT*

THERE
ENDS

*— in capital letters. This wall, and its message, is
built behind* CHARLIE, *who remains unaware.*
DOGG, *having put the ribbon up to his satisfaction,
turns round and sees the message.* ABLE *and*
BAKER *stand innocently behind the wall.* DOGG
looks at CHARLIE. CHARLIE *looks at the wall.*
CHARLIE *looks at* DOGG. CHARLIE *smiles a
hesitant smile.* DOGG *slaps* CHARLIE *lightly on
the cheek.* CHARLIE *opens his mouth to protest.*
DOGG *cuffs him heavily on the other cheek and
knocks* CHARLIE *through the wall, which
disintegrates.* DOGG *leaves.* CHARLIE *sits
wonderingly amid the debris*

CHARLIE   (*to himself*) Dog pout there ends????

*CHARLIE repeats this formula to himself but it
still makes no sense to him.* DOGG *re-enters
unrolling a red carpet as he does so. He unrolls the
carpet towards the bottom step of the platform,
and tidies it up. Meanwhile* ABLE *and* BAKER
*hastily re-build the wall, but this time different
sides of the pieces are facing front, so the message
says:—*

SHOUT
DOGG
PERT
NEED

The wall is built behind CHARLIE, *who watches*
DOGG. *As he leaves,* DOGG *notices the wall and
the new message. He looks at* CHARLIE. CHARLIE
looks at the wall. He looks at DOGG

CHARLIE   (*hopefully*) Pax!

DOGG *knocks him through the wall, which
disintegrates.* CHARLIE *sits among the debris as*
DOGG *leaves.* CHARLIE *shouts after* DOGG:

Yob!!

*A posy of flowers is thrown to him from that
direction.* CHARLIE *looks at it wonderingly*

91

Yob???

March music. CHARLIE gets up, and starts rehearsing the presentation of the posy, bowing, etc. ABLE and BAKER meanwhile re-build the wall, once more presenting a new face to the front:—

DONT
UPSET
DOGG
HERE

ABLE and BAKER stand to attention by the wall. CHARLIE stands in front of the wall. ABLE and BAKER wave their flags. BRICK's flag is poked from the wings and is also waved.

A LADY enters. She is quite young, formally dressed in very good clothes, modestly not glamorously. Perhaps she is the Queen, or perhaps the wife of the Chairman of the Governors. She is followed by a smirking DOGG who carries a cushion on which sits a pair of golden scissors.

The LADY walks along the red carpet, smiling at the cheers and the flags. The music continues.

The LADY sees CHARLIE standing to attention with the posy. She halts expectantly but CHARLIE continues to look straight ahead. DOGG fumes. Finally the LADY continues past CHARLIE. The LADY then sees the steps of the platform and is a bit taken aback — CHARLIE has not done a very good job, the whole thing being rather wobbly. DOGG glares at CHARLIE who looks straight ahead. The LADY smiles bravely and mounts the steps to the top of the platform. The music stops and she is ready to give her speech, which is written on a small piece of paper held in her gloved hand.

LADY   (*nicely*) Scabs, slobs, black yobs, yids, spicks, wops . . .

As one might say, "Your grace, ladies and gentlemen, boys and girls . . ."

Sad fact, brats pule puke crap-pot stink, spit; grow up dunces crooks; rank socks dank snotrags, conkers, ticks;

crib books, cock snooks, block bogs, jack off, catch pox
pick spots, scabs, padlocks, seek kicks kinks, slack: nick
swag, swig coke, bank kickbacks; frankly cant stick kids.

> DOGG *smirkingly offers her the scissors, which she
> takes, up, and with a flourish she cuts through the
> ribbon, saying:*

Sod the pudding club!

> *Cheers and music. The school song is sung, lustily,
> by DOGG, ABLE and BAKER. It consists of the
> words "Floreat Cane" repeated over and over to
> the tune of "Onward Christian Soldiers."*

> DOGG *leads the LADY back along the red carpet.
> They now face the wall and the message for the
> first time. The LADY notices the message and is
> slightly taken aback. She pauses. DOGG sees the
> message. The singing dwindles almost to silence,
> but DOGG starts it up again, and the LADY
> continues along the carpet. As she is about to pass
> CHARLIE, he steps into her path with the posy
> held out*

CHARLIE   (*respectfully*) Yob.

> *The LADY freezes and then accepts the posy.
> CHARLIE steps back out of her way. DOGG glares
> at CHARLIE. The LADY and DOGG leave.
> CHARLIE looks at the wall. DOGG re-enters and
> stands in front of CHARLIE. CHARLIE looks at
> DOGG. DOGG looks at the wall. CHARLIE
> dutifully hurls himself through the wall, which
> disintegrates. DOGG leaves*

(*furiously*) Stinkbog! Poxy crank!

BAKER   (*laughing*) Oblong socks!

ABLE   Bagwash!

BAKER   Biscuits.

CHARLIE   (*still shouting at DOGG'S exit*) Canting poncy creep!
> ABLE *picks up a cube from the platform, and by*

*way of dismantling the construction, tosses the
cube towards the wings, with a shout, "Brick!"*
CHARLIE *intercepts the cube and catches it, and
replaces it, saying, insistently, "Cube." CHARLIE
climbs up the steps and surveys the audience, while*
BAKER *and* ABLE *tidy up the fallen wall but do
not rebuild it.*

Three points only while I have the platform. Firstly, just
because it's been opened, there's no need to run amok
kicking footballs through windows and writing on the
walls. It's me who's got to keep this place looking new so
let's start by leaving it as we find it. Secondly, I can take
a joke as well as any man, but I've noticed a lot of language
about the place and if there's one thing I can't stand it's
language. I forget what the third point is.

BAKER *and* ABLE *look up at him.* CHARLIE *jerks
his head at them and they leave. Then* CHARLIE
*descends and rapidly puts the wall up. This time it
says:—*

*DOGGS
TROUPE
THE
END*

CHARLIE *leaves.*

*For a curtain call, the cast marches on stage in
single file, to music, and collect the flags from
the audience. They line up.*

Slab?

ALL   Slab!

(ALL *bow*)

Cube!

They turn and march off, the last one ABLE
shouting over his shoulder: "Brick!" BRICK
appears from the wings and follows them out

END

The Ragpickers
by Norman Smythe

The first performance of *The Ragpickers* was at The Ambiance
Lunch-Hour Theatre Club at The Almost Free Theatre, London W1,
on the 27th March 1972, with:
> Ritchie Stewart
> Donal Cox
> Rio Fanning

An Inter-Action Production designed by Gabriella Falk and
directed by ED Berman

Approximate playing time: 60 minutes

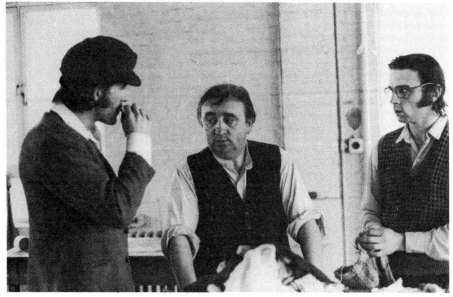

PHOTOGRAPH: INTER-ACTION

A room in the basement of a factory. In the centre of the room four long tables, or working benches, are set at right angles to each other so they form a hollow square. In one corner of the room the end of a steel chute is seen. At the opposite end of the room is an open lift, operated by a rope and pulley like a dumb waiter. There is a push button bell by the lift to give the signal to hoist.

Central heating pipes run through the room as do many ventilation shafts. The walls are covered with junction boxes from which cables run to the factory above. There is an old table and two chairs set against the wall. Nearby is another table with a gas ring on it. Beside it is a sink with one tap. The room has one entrance — through a four-panelled door. Screwed in this door is a coat hook upon which Tom's shabby raincoat is hung.

The play opens with TOM *at one of the benches sorting rags into two separate piles. On his right side, on the floor, is a sack half full of rags. At his left are two more sacks almost full into which he puts his sorting. All his movements are deliberate and quick through long practice. He has developed a certain routine from which he never deviates. He sings the first four lines of 'April in Portugal' and hums as he works.*

When he has finished sorting through the pile of rags on the bench he carefully stuffs the sorted rags into the two sacks on his left. Then there is the sound of a sack landing down chute. He notes this but goes to the sack on his right and carefully takes out three handfuls of rags and dumps them on the bench in a neat pile. Then he walks over to the chute, picks up the new sack on his back and carries it over to his bench and places it next to the sack he is working on. He then resumes sorting. TOM *is medium built, in his late forties and poorly dressed.*

There is a knock on the door. TOM *stops singing and cocks an ear then walks to the door.* JOE *is standing there. He is a small slightly built man, wearing glasses and is in his middle thirties. He wears a raincoat too big for him and a flat cap.*

96

TOM	I heard you the first time. I was busy.
JOE	Sorry. I didn't know. The Labour sent me. I'm to start here. *(Pause)* I was to ask for a feller called Tom.
TOM	That's me.
JOE	I'm to start here today they said.
TOM	Come on in then.
	JOE *enters.* TOM *closes door and walks back to bench.*
TOM	Take your coat off so, you can't work in it.
	JOE *removes his coat and looks vaguely around.*
JOE	Where will I put it?
TOM	(*looking around*) There's only the one coat hook here and that's mine. Hang it over there. (*indicating junction box*)
	JOE *hangs it on a corner of the box and returns.*
TOM	Ever do this work before?
JOE	No.
TOM	What did you do then?
JOE	Sweeping.
TOM	Sweeping. What kind of sweeping?
JOE	On the roads. I was with the Corporation.
TOM	What happened? Good steady money. Coming in regular.
JOE	The damp. The rain you see. The clinic says I should get inside out of the damp like. It's my chest. It gets at me something fierce.
TOM	There's sweeping up there. *(Jerking thumb in direction of ceiling)*

You'd think you'd want to stick to your own trade.

JOE   The Labour sent me here to sort rags.

TOM   Not that sweeping is really a trade you know.

JOE   It's steady enough working for the Corporation. If it wasn't for my chest . . . .

TOM   Sweeping isn't sorting. There's more to it than just pushing a broom. Not everyone has the knack.

JOE   The feller at the Labour said I'd learn it alright. Pick it up you know.

TOM   Pick it up! On your own? You have to have someone teach you. Did the feller at the Labour say anything about that now?

JOE   He said I'd pick it up alright. No bother. (*Pause*) I needed the job you see.

TOM   These fellers at the counter think they know everything. And what do they do? Make you sign on three times a week, stamp your card and fill in forms. They know bugger all about this job. I can tell you that for nothing.

                   Pause

JOE   If you could show me like.

                   There is the sound of another sack landing down the chute.

TOM   Jasus! Now what are they up to? I've only the one pair of hands. You'd think they'd show some bloody consideration.

                   Pause — looks at JOE

            You're wearing glasses.

JOE   But I've always worn them, you know. Ever since I was a kid. I can see alright with them.

TOM   It isn't sight you need for this job let me tell you. It's feel. You tell by the feel of the rags, you see. Not by looking.

Now you stand over there and watch me. Just watch me and don't say nothing. You can ask questions afterwards. You follow?

JOE   Yeh.

TOM   But first come over here.

> *They walk round the table until they can see the chute*

Now you go and get that sack and bring it here.

> JOE *walks over to the sack and starts to drag it to the workbench.*

No! Hump it on your shoulder!

> JOE *lifts it awkwardly on his shoulder.*

No! Get under it man. Did you never carry a sack of coal?

> JOE *drops the sack then bends down and picks it up again like a sack of coal. He staggers over to the bench with* TOM *watching him critically.*

I hope you'll be able for this job. That's the easy part. It's sorting where the real skill comes in.

> JOE *drops the sack beside the other.*

Now come on and watch me. We're after wasting time. And remember, no questions till I'm good and ready. Alright?

JOE   I'll remember.

TOM   What's your name?

JOE   Joe.

TOM   Joe eh. Alright Joe. Now I'll finish sorting this pile I got on bench. (*demonstrates*). Here goes wool and here goes cotton. (*he rapidly sorts through the pile*). Now I put the wool in here and the cotton in here. (*stuffing rags into open sacks on his left*).

	Now, you push down as hard as you can see. Tight. Got it?
JOE	Yeh. Yeh.
TOM	You want to try your hand at it now? Or do you want to watch me again?
JOE	How do you tell the wool from the cotton?
TOM	By the feel. (*gives JOE a rag*). What's that now?
JOE	Would it be wool?
TOM	Right first time. Lucky guess. Wool is thicker than cotton. Not always but most of the time. You can tell by the feel. Cotton's more slippy like. (*gives him two more rags.*) Now then, what's them?

> JOE *takes the rags. Feels them. Starts to speak. Hesitates.*

	Come on, we haven't got all day. Speak up man, what are they?
JOE	I think they're cotton.
TOM	Think! You've got to be certain sure, That's the job. That's what they're paying you for. Well, what are they?
JOE	I'd say they're cotton.
TOM	(*checking*) Cotton they are. Alright I'm going to let you have a go at sorting but I'm going to watch. Now get cracking. (*Takes handful of rags and dumps them on JOE's bench.*) Now, get on with it.

> JOE *starts to sort slowly.* TOM *watches critically. After JOE has sorted half a dozen* TOM *snatches a rag up.*

	What't that? What would you say that is?
JOE	(*feeling*) Wool?
TOM	Are you sure?

100

JOE	I think so. I mean I'm sure.
TOM	You'd better be sure. This isn't sweeping you know. Any old eejit with a broom can sweep. Well, is it wool or is it not?
JOE	It is Tom.
TOM	Then why the bloody hell did you put it on the cotton pile?
JOE	It was a mistake. I wasn't thinking.
TOM	Wasn't thinking! You wasn't thinking. But that's the job. I'm not paid to do your thinking for you. They don't like mistakes here. They raise holy hell if they find wool in the wrong sack. Alright now, put it in the right pile and get on with it.

> JOE *resumes sorting slowly.* TOM *checking occasionally.* JOE *holds out a rag.*

JOE	What's this? I'm not quite sure
TOM	What do you think it is?
JOE	I don't know. That's why I asked.
TOM	Well, give a guess. What would you say it is?
JOE	It feels like wool. But it's thin and slippy like.
TOM	It is wool. But I wouldn't call it slippy. Yes, it's wool alright.

> JOE *resumes sorting.*

	Alright. I've got my own work to do. Will you be okay on your own for a while?
JOE	I think so.
TOM	You're very slow. Ah well, keep at it. And for God's sake ask me if you're not sure. Do you hear?
JOE	Yeh. Yeh.

	TOM *returns to his own bench and deftly sorts his rags. They work in silence for a while.* TOM *stuffs his rags into the appropriate sacks.*
TOM	Come over here till I show you something.
	JOE *walks over.*
TOM	Now these sacks are full, see. They have to be sealed up.
	Takes a large needle and twine and sews mouths of sacks.
	Now this one is cotton and this one's wool. We know that but how will they know, eh?
JOE	I don't know Tom.
TOM	Well watch. I'll mark one of them. (*takes a can of whitewash and marks a cross on one of the sacks*). That's wool. You don't have to mark them both. They know the one with this cross here is wool. Follow?
JOE	Yeh. Tom.
TOM	Now for the last stage of the operation. Grab a hold of that sack will you.
	TOM *grabs one sack, lifts in on his shoulder and walks over to the lift.* JOE *follows with the other sack. They load them on the lift.*
	Now we give them the old signal.
	Presses button. We hear the bell ring and soon the lift goes up.
	There you are now. Job right!
JOE	That's handy alright.
TOM	It's all organized Joe. All thought out.
	Sound of sack dropping down chute.
	Holy Mary! They're going mad today. Go on Joe. Don't just stand there. Go and get the sack.

JOE goes and brings back the sack.

TOM You'll have to shift yourself. We're falling behind. I suppose when you first came in here — when you first walked through that door — you thought it was a soft job, eh, Be honest now. You thought there was nothing to it.

JOE They said I'd pick it up alright. I mean, I never done it before.

TOM You don't have to tell me that. It's as plain as the bloody nose on your face. But there's more to it than you thought. Go on. Admit it, Joe.

JOE It'll take a lot of getting used to alright.

TOM Different to sweeping?

JOE Like chalk and cheese.

TOM Alright so. Now, I've got to get back to the job. I've shown you all I can, have I not?

JOE You have, Tom.

TOM Well get on with it and cut out the blather.

> *TOM takes his place at his bench. They both continue to sort. JOE still works slowly but a little quicker than before. When he has finished his pile he calls to TOM.*

JOE I've finished this lot. Would you ever check it?

> *TOM checks it.*

TOM That's alright. No mistakes so far. But you've been taking long enough about it.

JOE Better sure than sorry Tom.

TOM Now go over there. (*Points*) There in the corner. You'll find some empty sacks. Bring two over here.

> *JOE does so.*

Now open them up like this.

Shows how the mouths of the sacks are left open.

Alright. Now we're ready to start filling these. Now you put more rags on the bench yourself. Not too many. Say, three handfuls.

> JOE *arranges a new pile of rags on his bench and they resume work.* JOE *is now working a little quicker.*

TOM   You always do sweeping?

JOE   I worked up at the brewery once. St. James's Gate.

TOM   Did you now. That'd be a good billet I'd say. What were you doing, sampling the pints?

JOE   In the bottling department.

TOM   What happened you?

JOE   The work was a bit heavy like.

TOM   You got laid off.

JOE   I got laid off.

TOM   What else you done?

JOE   I worked in Murphy's pub in Ringsend.

TOM   Barman?

JOE   Not in the union. Just helping out. Collecting the glasses, washing them, you know. Weekends.

TOM   You'd need more than that to keep you going.

JOE   I used to deliver for a grocery on Grafton Street during the week but they went out of business.

TOM   On a bike?

JOE	Yeh. On a bike with a big carrier in front. I liked that. Look, I finished Tom.
TOM	(*checks pile*) Right. All in proper order. Now you can put them in the sacks yourself. Don't make a mistake now. This one's the wool. (*indicating*)

JOE stuffs rags in sacks.

TOM	(*checking pocket watch*) It's just about dinner time. I'll put the kettle on.

> *He lights the gas ring. Fills the kettle from the one tap at the brown sink. Puts it on the flame. They both resume work.*

JOE	You been here a long time Tom?
TOM	Long enough. I'm on steady. Paid by the week. I'm not casual you know.
JOE	Oh I figured that alright. It's a nice enough job. Bit hard on the old pins standing all day. Too bad there isn't a couple of stools.
TOM	You want it too soft altogether. Sitting wouldn't be right. You've got to stay alert. You need your wits about you for this job.
JOE	I'll manage alright. I've had too more than a few jobs in my time you know.
TOM	This is a standing up job, Joe.
JOE	And I never had no trouble learning the work. I just packed up the jobs — when I felt like it. Not because I couldn't do it.
TOM	Fair enough. I was just telling you the rules. That's what I'm here for.
JOE	I didn't think there'd be any harm in sitting on a stool every once in a while. I never meant all the time.
TOM	Let me put it to you this way, if the gaffers upstairs (*pointing up*) thought the job called for stools they would

have put them in here, right?

JOE   I suppose so. Still and all . . . . .

TOM   It's all organized, Joe. All thought out. You'll get used to it.

JOE   (*Pause*) Where's that steam coming from?

TOM   There's a boiler over there making steam for the works up there (*pointing*). Some of it leaks out like when the pressure's up.

JOE   I don't think it'll be too good for my chest. (*coughs*)

TOM   Go way out of that, man. It's the dry air that grabs you in the throat.

JOE   It's the chest you see, the damp . . . . . .

TOM   Damp is it? This place is as dry as a bone. You don't know when you're well off. Many's a feller I've heard complaining about being crucified with the cold in some of those old factories. But not here, eh Joe?

JOE   If you think it's alright.

TOM   Amn't I telling you that there's no harm in that bit of steam at all but just the opposite. It'll do you all the good in the world — especially if you're prone to a bit of weakness in the old box (*tapping chest*).

JOE   Well, if you say so Tom.

The factory whistle blows.

TOM   There you are! Dinner time and the kettle should be ready.

The kettle starts to sing. They both stop work. TOM goes to his coat and takes out a paper bag of sandwiches and a carton of milk.

You bring something to eat Joe?

JOE   I've a couple of sandwiches.

He gets them from his raincoat and they both sit down at the table. TOM *sets out two cups and saucers and makes the tea.*

TOM How long did you say you were here for?

JOE A couple of weeks, maybe three.

TOM Well, you can use my tea this week. Next week you can chip in if you like.

JOE I'll pay you for the tea and the milk this week, soon as I get paid.

TOM Be better if you bought it next week. How much sugar?

JOE Four spoonfuls. I like it sweet like.

TOM Right you are. What kind of sandwiches do you have?

JOE Jam. Strawberry jam.

TOM I've got one cheese and one corned beef. You can have half the corned beef if you like.

JOE I wouldn't rob you Tom.

TOM Go on man. Take it. (*offers a sandwich.*)

JOE And I'll give you half of one of mine. Do you care for jam?

TOM It's alright. Makes a change.

> *They both eat.* TOM *quickly and noisily.* JOE *slowly and quietly.*

Live at home Joe?

JOE Not now. Since the Mammy died I stayed with the sister. But she got married last year.

TOM You're on your tod so.

JOE I've a room in a house off Talbot Street.

TOM That's very handy for you. Do you get out much?

JOE	Where?
TOM	Out. Into town. To the flicks. The pubs.
JOE	I'm not much at drinking. A pint or so weekends.
TOM	No family?
JOE	Only the sister. And she's married now and living in Carlow.
TOM	Well, you have somewhere to visit. A trip down the country.
JOE	Yeh. I'll have to go down someday.
TOM	It'd be nice. Make a change.
JOE	Yeh. (*pause*) What about you Tom, are you married?
TOM	I was. I lost the missus — going on ten years ago now.
JOE	Any kids?
TOM	No. We never had any. Used to keep pigeons though. We rented our own house. Very nice.
JOE	Still got it?
TOM	It was too big, you know, just for me. I live with the brother and his wife now.
JOE	You've got company so.
TOM	It's not like you think. The place full of kids. Now the eldest is getting on and wants his own room. Begob, I wish he had it too. Him and his old guitar. I'll have to move out.
JOE	Guitar?
TOM	Always at it, screeching and moaning, and him only fourteen.
JOE	It's nice all the same. When you can play proper, that is.

TOM   You wouldn't say that if you could hear him at it.
Always on about the Hills of Tennessee and him never been
further than the Hill of Howth.

JOE   I always fancied playing the guitar meself.

TOM   You never!

JOE   I did so, or the melodeon. It'd be nice alright, all the
people standing round listening, joining in the chorus, like.

TOM   Fair enough if you've the talent for it. I like a bit of music
meself. Always did. But this feller now, he has no ear for
music at all. And a voice on him like an old donkey with
asthma.

JOE   You'll miss the company, all the same.

TOM   I won't. Be my own boss. Get a nice room somewhere,
handy to town. Cook what I want and eat when I want.
I've got a good steady job. Shouldn't be too hard to find a
decent room somewhere.

JOE   I'd say you're fond of the odd pint now and then.

TOM   Why do you say that?

JOE   I saw the way you looked when I said I used work at the
brewery. Like it would have suited you.

TOM   I like the occasional pint alright. Play the odd game of darts.
More for the company you know than the booze. But I
keep pretty much to myself.

JOE   But you've company at home.

TOM   It's not like that I tell you. Always having to move when
the sister-in-law wants to get on with the housework. Can't
get settled. Kids running in and out all the time. Doors
always banging. Can't settle down to read the paper, never
mind watching the telly.

JOE   Telly. You've got a telly. That's grand. You'll miss that.

TOM	And what's to stop me renting one on my own. By the week. I've got steady money coming in. There'd be no bother about that.
JOE	No. There'd be no bother about that. Just sign your name. It's well for you, Tom, in a good steady job like this. Permanent.
TOM	That's what it is. Permanent. I don't know if there's a pension in it. I never asked. But I've saved a few quid you know, for the rainy day.
JOE	You're pretty well fixed. I wish . . . .
TOM	Now Joe, don't feel bad. Maybe they'll keep you on longer than the fortnight. Maybe they'll get really busy and need an extra man. Steady.
JOE	They said two weeks, maybe three at the most.
TOM	But what the hell do them fellers know. They know nothing. We're busy enough now and maybe we'll stay busy. Who knows. Look on the bright side.
JOE	I always did Tom. My Mammy said I was always the cheerful one.
TOM	Well, there you are then. And if you're not kept on here maybe you'll get a steady job somewhere else — an inside job away from the damp.
JOE	I'll look on the bright side, Tom.
TOM	That's the idea. (*pause*) Ever go to the zoo, Joe?
JOE	The zoo?
TOM	Yeh, you know, Phoenix Park.
JOE	I used to go with my Mammy and Bridie, the sister.
TOM	I go just about every Sunday. I like looking at the flamingoes. Then I have a bite to eat in the café.

JOE	That'd make a nice day out.
TOM	It does. And you'd spend more on having a few jars in the local. It doesn't cost all that much.
JOE	When I get paid . . . . . .
TOM	Yeh?
JOE	As soon as I get a few bob I'd like to go.
TOM	You mean it?
JOE	I would. Honest to God. I'd like to see the lions and monkeys. And the flamingoes of course. Is them the birds that bury themselves in the sands up to their necks?
TOM	Them's ostriches. You can see them as well. Queer looking beasts they are too. No, flamingoes is pink. They've long legs and long necks alright but when they move about it's like they're doing a slow dance. Ostriches are a different kettle of fish altogether. They're clumsy and ugly. You should see those flamingoes, Joe, when the sun's shining. All pink and graceful like among the green grass. It's a sight worth seeing I can tell you.
JOE	What would they eat?
TOM	I don't know. Bits of things in the grass or in the water. Worms maybe. I don't know. But if you should see them lifting up their legs when they walk and their neck stretched out (*pause*) Do you mean it, Joe?
JOE	What?
TOM	About going?
JOE	I do surely. As soon as I get the readies. I'll go this weekend. This Sunday. Maybe I could meet you and you could show me around. I mean, you must know the place pretty well.
TOM	None better. I know all the keepers by sight. To nod to you know. I've got pretty pally with the keeper in the reptile house. His name is Peter. We often have a regular old chat about snakes. Very interesting too.

111

JOE   That's very decent of you Tom.

TOM   What?

JOE   Letting me go along with you.

TOM   Not at all. I'll be glad of the company. Some more tea?

JOE   If there's any left.

TOM   Plenty for both of us. (*pours*) Right. That's settled so. This Sunday. We can make the arrangements later.

       The whistle blows. TOM *gulps down his tea.*

       Go on. You finish your cuppa. I'll get on with the job. You take your time.

       He rinses his cup and goes back to the bench and resumes work. JOE *finishes his tea. Rinses his cup and goes to his bench. They work away steadily.* TOM *hums and sings the Blue Danube. After a few beats* JOE *joins him by whistling.* TOM *glances across at* JOE.

       You're getting the hang of it nicely now. I'd say you really have the knack for this work.

JOE   Thanks Tom, it's coming along a little better now.

TOM   You're picking it up almost as fast as I did. When I started here ten years ago there were three of us. All temporary. When things got slack they laid off the other two fellers and kept me on.

JOE   You've been here ten years so.

TOM   Almost to the day.

JOE   And before that? You don't mind me asking?

TOM   (*pause*) I've never told anyone before. The brother knows. Of course. I was in a different class of trade altogether. I was a turner and . . . .

JOE   What's that Tom?

TOM   Working on a lathe. Served me time five years. It's a good
         trade Joe, the best there is. You have to know what you're
         about in a machine shop.

JOE   The money would be good I'd say.

TOM   One of the highest paid trades there is. I was renting like I
         told you but I had my eye on a house in Santry with a nice
         bit of a garden.

JOE   What happened you so?

TOM   I was a bit too fond of the old jar. Went on the skite once
         too often. I knew I'd be for the high jump if I stayed off the
         job again so I went in of the Monday when I still had the
         shakes.

JOE   Ah, drink's a curse, so it is.

TOM   To make a long story short I made a regular bags of the job
         I was on — special kind of shaft that was worth a packet. I
         could never get a job in my own trade after.

JOE   We all have our troubles Tom. But you're well fixed now.
         A nice steady job.

TOM   Yeh. I pulled myself together after I lost the missus. And I
         never take more than the odd jar now.

JOE   A pity about your old job all the same. I mean, after you
         serving your time and all.

TOM   A job is what a man makes it. There's a lot to this one like
         I've told you. And I'm my own boss like. I'm in charge.

JOE   I can understand now how you have the knack of it. You
         know, after having been a turner and everything. But I'll
         never get it.

TOM   Sure you will. It's just practice.

JOE   No. Not in a month of Sundays.

TOM   Well, if you don't do quite as good as me you'll be treading
         on my heels.

113

JOE   You think so Tom?

TOM   I'm sure of it. It's a gift and I think you've got it Joe.

                          They work in silence for a while.

            What's that room like of yours?

JOE   Not so hot. Why?

TOM   Well, I'll be looking for a room like I told you. I thought maybe if there was one going vacant in your house?

JOE   It wouldn't suit a man like you Tom. Not one who's been used to his own house, and pigeons and everything. It's not up to much. Small and dark.

TOM   I'm sorry to hear that.

JOE   If I got steady work again I'd move out. Maybe near the sea. Then I could come in on a bike.

TOM   You have a bike then?

JOE   No. But I could buy one on the never never. If I had a steady job that is.

TOM   If you don't get taken on here steady I could keep my eyes and ears open for you. How about that now?

JOE   That's very good of you Tom.

TOM   Did you ever try the buses?

JOE   I wouldn't be able for the stairs. Not up and down all day. Besides I'd be scared out of my wits handling all that money.

TOM   Well, there's lots of jobs going Joe. I'll look out for you. (*pause. Looks at him critically.*) You need to eat more. Meat and potatoes every day. You need more weight on you. There's not much nourishment in jam sandwiches.

JOE   I get a good feed pretty often at a café near the house.

TOM   Sausage and chips. I know them places. Not like a home cooked meal Joe. I'll tell you one thing Joe, the missus was only a grand cook. Cook anything she could but her speciality was meat puddings. I always said she could have opened her own café serving nothing else.

JOE   You're right there. The sister was only a wonderful cook. Make a real tasty meal she could.

TOM   There's not much joy in living on your own. And that's a fact.

JOE   You never said a truer word Tom. And yet you come and go as you please. All the quiet you want to read the papers or to have a bit of a snooze like.

Two more bags come down the chute.

Two of them! Let's go Joe.

They move to retrieve the sacks.

The pressure's on, boy. I'm glad you're here to help.

At the bench again

TOM   It looks like it could be good news tonight. If there's more than two sacks unopened at knocking off time we're entitled to stay and do overtime. That's the rules. Sometimes there's two hours in it. At time and a half.

JOE   That's great.

TOM   That'll pay your way into the zoo — and enough to buy your lunch. Plus a bag of buns for the elephants. What do you think of that?

JOE   Smashing. *(pause)* I hope I'll be able for it Tom. My legs are aching a bit.

TOM   Now never mind about that. Amn't I here? I'll lend you a hand. I'll see you alright. Never fear.

They resume work.

You know, Joe, I've never taken any one home — for a bit of supper like. No reason why I shouldn't. I pay my whack. Regular. *(pause)* Would you like to come back with me one night?

115

JOE	*(pause)* I wouldn't want to put your sister-in-law to any trouble.
TOM	What trouble is in it now? I bet you don't eat more than a sparrow. *(pause)* We could have a pint or two on the way home. Work up an appetite.
JOE	Thanks Tom all the same. But leave it over a bit will you?
TOM	Whatever you say Joe. No rush.
	Pause
	Be no harm if I took a dekko at the papers. Maybe I'd find a room that would suit us both. Near the sea eh?
JOE	I often wished I'd been a sailor. The sea's the place.
TOM	And sharing with someone you get on with is the thing I'd say. It's company. Many's the time I feel like a bit of a chat after reading something in the papers.
JOE	Or about a game in Dalymount Park.
TOM	That's it. A pint and a chat after the game is the best part. Do you watch soccer Joe?
JOE	I always meant to go. A feller took me to Shelbourne Park once.
TOM	Nothing like a night out at the dogs. Now if we shared a room we could arrange all sorts of trips. God, there wouldn't be enough time left in the world to do all the things we wanted to do, eh?
JOE	You're right there, Tom.
	They work in silence for a while. JOE *leaning his elbows on the bench as he works.*
TOM	How's the legs?
JOE	Alright.
TOM	Take a breather. Go over and sit at the table for ten minutes. No-one will know.

JOE	I'm alright, Tom.
TOM	You'll get used to it. It takes getting used to. After all, this is only your first day. It must be hard on you. I mean, you're used to sweeping. Being on the move all the time. Right?
JOE	That's right Tom.
TOM	You'll get used to it in no time. In a month you'll be doing it automatic like. And then you can think of other things. I often think about when I was a kid going to school. (*laughs*) The teacher, Miss Molloy, used to poke through our hair with a pencil, looking for nits.
JOE	I don't think I'll get used to it at all. Ever.
TOM	Stop you talking! You will of course.
JOE	(*low*) I won't, Tom.
TOM	Why? Why do you say that?
JOE	I appreciate what you're doing alright. But it's no use.
TOM	What do you mean. No use?
JOE	Nothing
TOM	You must mean something. You can't say things that mean nothing. (*looks at him*)

Huh? It doesn't make sense. |
JOE	I know. That's just it.
TOM	What?
JOE	I won't be able to stick it. Now leave me alone, will you.

> *They work in silence.* JOE *starts to speak several times.* TOM *sees this but waits.*

I can't stick at anything and that's the gospel truth. It wasn't only on account of my chest I left the Corporation. I couldn't stick it any longer. I've had dozens of jobs —

117

maybe hundreds. I just can't stick at them. And that's the truth. Now you know.

TOM   But you could change. I mean, a nice job like this. Warm and dry and steady money and all.

JOE   It wouldn't work Tom. I know. I'll never change. You could ask the sister. She got fed up with me. That's why she moved out and got married. There was no need.

TOM   But you could try to stick it this time. You don't know until you try, do you now? Eh?

JOE   I don't know, Tom.

TOM   But isn't that what I'm after saying. You don't know until you try. Look at Napoleon!

JOE   Napoleon?

TOM   Yeh, Napoleon. He didn't know what he could do until he tried. He failed over and over again and then he succeeded. He kept on trying, Joe. Keep thinking of Napoleon. Eh?

JOE   I don't know much about him to tell you the truth. I've heard of him of course.

TOM   I've told you all you need to know about him. He stuck at it. Like the spider in the cave he watched when he was in exile, he kept on trying. He wouldn't give up.
I wish I'd seen the film. Maybe if it comes round again we could go and see it together.

       The door bursts open and FERGUS *enters. He is a burly man in his mid thirties with a stupid, crafty face. He wears his cheap clothes with a certain swagger. His coat is belted and his cap is at a rakish angle.* JOE *looks at him with interest.*

FERGUS The Labour sent me. I gave my cards to the gaffer upstairs in the office. (*to* JOE) Sorting rags is it?

JOE   Yeh. Tom here will show you . . . .

       FERGUS *takes off his coat vigorously, looks*

around. Walks back to the door and hangs his hat
and coat over TOM's *raincoat which falls to the*
floor. FERGUS *moves to the bench.*

TOM   Watch it feller! Watch what you're doing now!

FERGUS   (*belligerently.*) What's that? What are you on about mate?

TOM   My coat. You knocked my coat down.

            FERGUS *hesitates then goes back to the door and*
            roughly hangs up TOM's *coat over his. Then he*
            approaches JOE.

FERGUS   Alright, what do we do eh?

TOM   The sacks come down . . .

FERGUS   I wasn't asking you.

JOE   But Tom's the boss here. He knows . . .

FERGUS   (*examining* JOE's *pile of rags*) What are you sorting, cotton
            from wool?

JOE   That's right but . . . .

TOM   I'll tell him Joe. (*to* FERGUS) You go over to the chute
            see . . . . . .

            FERGUS *picks up full sack, rips it open and dumps*
            contents on bench.

            That's not the way to do it!

FERGUS   What is it then?

TOM   You take three handfuls. Place them on the bench . . .

FERGUS   (*starting to sort*) Alright. So I took ten handfuls, twenty
            maybe. What's the differ, eh?

            TOM *motions to* JOE *to move closer to him.* JOE
            does so.

TOM	(*low*) Let him alone. He won't be here for long. I can tell you that for nothing.
JOE	It's a wonder he doesn't want to learn to do the job properly.
TOM	An ignorant lot altogether. I know his type.
FERGUS	(*stopping work.*) What's that whispering! Are you talking about me? (*moves threateningly to* TOM) Because if you are I'll give you a puck in the gob in short order, mate. Make no mistake about that.

Returns to his own bench.

JOE	(*low*) Don't bother about him Tom. Let him alone.
TOM	A bowsie. An ignorant, good for nothing bowsie. That's what he is.
JOE	Sh!
FERGUS	Now I warned you. Don't say I didn't (*grabs handfuls of sorted rags. To* JOE) Where do I put these? They're cotton.
JOE	Tom will tell you.
FERGUS	I'm asking you. I won't ask twice.
JOE	(*hastily*) Here. In this sack.

FERGUS *stuffs cotton in the sack indicated and then the pile of wool in the other sack.*
TOM *goes to the sack and examines the rags. He walks over to* FERGUS *with one rag in his hand.*

TOM	Cotton. This is cotton.
FERGUS	I can see it's cotton. What about it?
TOM	You put it in the sack with the wool.
FERGUS	(*snatches it out of his hand and goes over to cotton sack and drops it in*) What differ does one lousy old rag make?

TOM   You're paid to sort. That's what you're here for.

FERGUS   Don't come that with me mate. I'm warning you.

TOM   Listen you! I work here regular. Steady. I'm not a casual, by the hour. This is my job and I'm in charge. If you want to work here tomorrow you'd better remember that.

Looks at FERGUS *steadily then goes back to his place.* JOE *gives him an approving look.* TOM *goes to pile of empty sacks in corner picks up two and drops them by* FERGUS. *Marks one with a cross.*

Now, them are your sacks. The one with a cross is for the wool. See you don't make any more mistakes.

FERGUS   Frig off will you!

They work in silence. FERGUS *looking occasionally across at* JOE.

TOM   *(low)* I could have a word with the sister-in-law tonight. Maybe on pay night we could . . .

JOE   I told you Tom, I'm not good in company. I get nervous eating with strangers. I never know what to say.

TOM   Right. I know a caff. Near the quays. They put out a good feed. Reasonable. Plenty of meat and potatoes. How would that suit you?

JOE   Sounds good.

TOM   Well, will we make it a date then? Straight after work.

FERGUS   *(looking around)* Is there not a stool in this bloody place?

JOE   No, you see it wouldn't be right to . . . .

TOM   Don't talk to him Joe. Let him alone.

FERGUS   What do you mean it wouldn't be right? Why not? *(lights a cigarette)*

TOM   No smoking in here.

121 FERGUS   I don't see no sign.

TOM   No smoking except during tea breaks.

FERGUS   Well, I'm taking my break now. Alright.

                TOM resumes work.

           Yeh, a stool would be just the job. (*to* JOE) Hey haven't I seen you down at the Labour, signing on?

TOM   Don't answer him Joe.

FERGUS   I remember you now. Your name is Joe something. Right?

                JOE nods.

TOM   Ignore him.

FERGUS   You were talking to the feller behind the counter. The one. with the glasses who gave you the card for here. He's a good pal of mine. Gets me lots of jobs.

                Walks to JOE and shakes his hand

           My name is Fergus.

JOE   Hi!

FERGUS   *(resuming work)* He's going to fix me up in a good job next week . . . . .

TOM   Watch that fag. These rags are inflammable.

                FERGUS throws cigarette on floor and stamps on it with a flourish. Winks at JOE

TOM   *(sews up bag and hands paint pot to JOE)* Here, you can mark the sack if you like.

                JOE does so

           Next time you can sew the bags up yourself.

JOE   Thanks, Tom.

TOM   Then you will have done everything. The whole operation. That's not bad for your first day on the job, is it now?

JOE	No Tom.

They walk over to the lift.

TOM	You see, Joe, you're willing to learn, to do the job proper. Not like some. You've got to have pride in your work. Right?
JOE	Right.
TOM	How's the legs?
JOE	Fair enough Tom. Grand.
TOM	(*loading the sacks onto the lift*) Now, you ring the bell.

JOE *does so.* TOM *listens with satisfaction. As they walk back to the bench* TOM *moves* JOE *to the other side so* JOE *is now at the bench to his left.*

You work this side, alright?

TOM *is now working between* JOE *and* FERGUS. FERGUS *glares at him while he sorts carelessly.*

Watch it now! I've told you before. Don't mix them up.

FERGUS	Ah, what's the differ eh! Who cares if you mix them up a bit?
TOM	It's the job. I told you.
FERGUS	It's no job at all. Not for a man, that is. Ragpicking! Only fitting for women.
JOE	If you'd take the trouble to learn the job proper ....
TOM	Quiet Joe! It's not ragpicking, it's sorting.
JOE	There's a knack to it.
FERGUS	Who're you codding. Knack! Sure a child of ten could do it — with its eyes closed.

Closes his eyes and elaborately sorts, tossing rags in the air.

See.

JOE *laughs.* TOM *hushes him.*

TOM   It's well to see you won't be here for long.

JOE   You won't be kept on steady.

FERGUS   I wouldn't want to ke kept on here steady. Not if I was
           blind and crippled and starving. It's no job for a man. I
           don't work at nothing steady. Come and go as I please. I'm
           my own man. Listen.

           *He moves his piles of rags to the next bench to his
           right so that he is next to* JOE.

           Do you know what I was doing last summer eh? Give a guess.

JOE   I don't know.

TOM   And we're not interested.

FERGUS   Fruit picking. Over beyond in England. There was hundreds
           of students. Some smashing birds. You shoulda seen one I
           was knocking around with. Swedish, she was. Took a real
           fancy to me. Used to buy me pints in the local. And what
           do you think she did when she left. You know, at the end
           of the season when the job was over?
           Give a guess Joe.

JOE   I don't know.

FERGUS   Give me a fiver — for services rendered. (*laughs*)

TOM   (*low*) Don't mind him. Get on with your work Joe. You're
           doing fine. How the legs?

FERGUS   He needs a bloody stool, same as me.

TOM   I wasn't talking to you. Get on with your work and keep
           to yourself.

           Pause. They work.

FERGUS   Hey! Is that steam escaping?

JOE   Yeh. No harm in it though.

FERGUS	Live steam! Hey Boss, did you know the air is being polluted?

JOE *coughs*

TOM	Get on with your work and not be bothering about a bit of steam.
JOE	It's good for you. Isn't that right, Tom?
FERGUS	Good for you! Do you know what I'm going to tell you. I could get the Health Department to close the whole shebang here like that. (*snaps fingers*) One phone call from me and everybody out.
JOE	All the same Fergus, it's warm. There's some fellers crucified with the cold and . . . .
FERGUS	Now if I had a stilson wrench, some compound and lagging I could fix that up in a jiffy. I used to work for a plumber you know.
TOM	We have our own maintenance crew here so just forget it.
FERGUS	Well, see you get them down here or . . .

Makes dialling motion and winks at JOE. *They resume work*

I bet you don't know what these rags are used for, eh? I bet you don't know. I bet you a hundred quid.

TOM *concentrates on his work.*

JOE	Tell him Tom.
FERGUS	He can't tell because he doesn't know. I won my bet.
TOM	The job here is sorting. That's my job. And teaching the casuals. That's my job too. Them's that willing to learn, that is.
FERGUS	You don't know! Well, I do. I've used them. Many and many a time. The cotton's used for polishing cars and things. And the wool is used in machine shops for mopping up the oil. You know, around the lathes and such like. I've used

them both. So what the hell does it matter if you get one or
two mixed up? Nothing! It doesn't matter a tinker's damn.
Nobody notices.

TOM   The gaffer upstairs will have a different notion about that,
I can tell you. You'll get your cards tomorrow.

FERGUS   So what! I'll be in another job by dinner time. No bother.
Maybe I'll go down the country. (*to* JOE) Do you know I
was with a circus once?

JOE   (*interested*) Yeh?

FERGUS   For a year. Almost. Travelled every parish in Ireland.
Putting up the tents the booths and assembling the seats.
Hard graft it was too. A man's job I can tell you. Not like
this. Women's work.

JOE   What happened. Why did you leave?

TOM   Don't listen to him. It's only a pack of lies.

FERGUS   Lies is it! Calling me a liar are you! You want to have a bet
on it? You go and ask anybody at O'Malley's circus if
Fergus wasn't with them. They'll tell you. Ah, what do you
know about anything anyway. Spent your whole life in this
shagging kip ragpicking.

JOE   That's not true! Tom has . . .

TOM   Never mind him.

JOE   But tell him you had your own house and all.

FERGUS   A corner in a public house is more like it.

TOM   I wouldn't waste my breath talking to that bowsie and I'd
advise you not to either.

FERGUS   And that's not all Joe. I was with the animals. The lions.

TOM   Here, let me check your work.

              Checks his piles

JOE   They're alright Tom.

FERGUS	Yeh. The lions. Proper fierce they were too. Not doped or anything, you know.
JOE	Gosh! Tom here goes to the zoo regular. Don't you Tom?
TOM	Ah, don't be believing a word this feller says. Lions!
FERGUS	I told you before mate. Ask anybody at O'Malley's. I wouldn't cod you Joe. Want to hear how I got the job helping with the animals?
JOE	Tom, there'd be no harm . . . . ?
TOM	It's up to you Joe. I can't tell you what to do. But I'd think you'd have more sense than . . . .
FERGUS	The regular feller who helped the trainer — his name was Lenihan — got sick. He was in the rats. You know, after too much booze. And because I was always interested, always watching them being fed, I got the job while he was drying out in Dublin. For three weeks.
JOE	What did you do?
FERGUS	Helped to feed them. Once a day. Pushed big hunks of meat through the bars. We had two lions a tiger and a bear. Then we had to get them from the cages into the ring. And back again. They'd roar and snarl something shocking when they had to go in the big cage in the ring but they'd run back to their own cages like lambs.
JOE	Were you ever scared?
FERGUS	No. What was there to be scared about. I used to poke at them with a stick to hurry them along. They're animals aren't they? We've got the brains. The old head power. It's them that was afraid of us.
JOE	Gosh! So why did you leave?
FERGUS	Ah well, there's a story there alright. I'll tell you sometime, Joe. I'm afraid it might shock your man there.
TOM	We don't want any of that sort of talk in here.

FERGUS   See! What did I tell you? Ah well, I would have moved on anyway. I don't like staying anywhere too long.

JOE   You mean you don't want steady work!

TOM   He couldn't keep a job for more than a few months. That's easy enough to see.

FERGUS   Wrong again me old segocia. Wrong again. I was working in a lumber yard in Limerick once and the boss begged me to stay on. Said he'd make me foreman. Not for me! I've been a gaffer in my time though you might not believe it.

TOM   We wouldn't.

FERGUS   Unloading coal at a siding in Arklow. There's back breaking work for you. Takes a man to handle a shovel full of coal right.

>   *Fills his two sacks. To* TOM

What do I do with these?

TOM   *(sewing them up)* Put them on the lift over there. *(points)*

>   FERGUS *grabs both sacks under his arms and takes them to the lift.* JOE *helps him to load them on.*

JOE   Will I ring the bell, Tom?

TOM   Go ahead. I don't see why he shouldn't do it himself. If he can tame a pack of lions I can't see why he can't ring his own bloody bell.

FERGUS   I never said I was a lion tamer. All I said was I helped the trainer. Right Joe?

JOE   Yeh. *(to* TOM*)* You have to be fair Tom, he never . . . .

TOM   Ah, shut up! Sorry Joe. I didn't mean it. That feller gets on my wick, that's all.

>   *They resume work.*

Did you say you were thinking of going down to Carlow to see the sister?

JOE	She asked me down alright but . . . .
TOM	But what, Joe?
JOE	I think she was only asking you know. We had a bit of a barney before she left.
TOM	But that's all dead and gone now. She'd be pleased to see you I'm sure.
JOE	You think so Tom?
TOM	Why wouldn't she so? Blood's thicker than water, you know. And who can you trust if you can't trust relations — and friends eh?
JOE	True enough Tom.
TOM	A day out in the country would do you the world of good. I could go down with you. Oh, I wouldn't go with you to your sister's. I could have a pint or two while you visited. I'd enjoy the bus ride.
JOE	That'd be nice alright. (*pause*) Were you ever in Killarney, Tom?
TOM	I was. Years ago when I was a kid.
JOE	Maybe we could go there on the bus and I could visit the sister some other time.
TOM	Fair enough.
FERGUS	Would you ever check these for me Tom? (*indicating piles*)
TOM	Why?
FERGUS	Just to make sure I've got them in the right piles. You're the boss.
TOM	Aren't you just after saying that it doesn't matter?
JOE	Do it for him, Tom. He wants to do it the proper way now.
TOM	Ah Janey Mac! Can't you see . . . .

129

He checks FERGUS's *work quickly then goes back to his own bench.*

FERGUS   All okay Tom?

TOM   Yeh.

        FERGUS *grins and winks at* JOE.

FERGUS   I was in Killarney once. Worked for the Council. On the roads. All summer. I bet you I seen more of the lakes and scenery than any shagging tourist.

JOE   I'll say you did. I worked for the Corporation once. Sweeping.

FERGUS   Is that right. So did I. Just for a week to fill in. In Rathmines. Rained every bloody day. I packed it in.

JOE   It's hard in winter alright.

FERGUS   How long were you at it?

JOE   Over three years.

FERGUS   You stuck it that long! Me, I wouldn't want anything that steady.

JOE   It all depends.

FERGUS   On what?

JOE   What you're doing. A steady job you know, a good job somewhere . . .

TOM   That's right Joe. Security. That's what you want.

FERGUS   Security me eye! Not for me. I like to come and go as I please. I'm my own man. I thought of going to Australia once.

JOE   Australia! Did you not go?

FERGUS   I could have. As easy as snapping my fingers. There was a feller wanted to give me the loan of the money but I changed my mind.

JOE	Were you ever in Australia Tom?
TOM	I would have told you if I was.
JOE	That's right Tom, you would have.
FERGUS	Remember that job I was telling you about? — the feller at the Labour is fixing me up with?
JOE	Yeh.
FERGUS	You'd like it.
TOM	He has a good job here. Right Joe?
JOE	That's right Tom.
FERGUS	This is a factory doing assembly work. You don't have to be in the union. It's easy work, sitting down and the pay is good.
TOM	You wouldn't want to work in one of them big factories. Some foreman watching you all the time. Speed ups and things like that.
FERGUS	What's wrong with a big factory? They've their own canteen. A good feed at dinner time, dirt cheap. Always lots of people to have a bit of crack with. You don't work as hard as you do here. And there's always lots of birds. Some of them dead easy.
TOM	That's just the sort of place Joe wouldn't want to work in.
JOE	I like a bit of company — now and then. And sitting down.
TOM	Now, if it's only a stool that's after bothering you.
FERGUS	They'll be taking on half a dozen men. I could put in a quiet word for you if you want.
TOM	He's not interested. He has a good job with the chance of being steady.
FERGUS	I'm not talking to you mate. I'm talking to Joe. How about it Joe?

131

JOE	I don't know.
TOM	But you do know. You know when you're well off.
JOE	I wouldn't want to work in a factory — not for long.
FERGUS	Janey Mac! Who says it'd be for long. It's only a month. That's why the pay is so good. It's temporary. I wouldn't want it for longer than a month. Not with summer coming on.
JOE	Summer?
FERGUS	Yeh. Summer's no time for working inside in shagging dumps like this. (*gestures*) I know a bloke in South Kerry who'd give us a start.
JOE	Would you be going near Killarney?
FERGUS	And why not? I'm my own man. I've got connections there. Ah yes, they all remember Fergus in Killarney.
TOM	The Guards too I bet. Now listen to me, Joe . . . .
FERGUS	No reason you couldn't come along with me. We could stop over in Killarney a few days. As long as we liked.
TOM	You wouldn't be able for it Joe. Travelling is terrible hard on your legs.
FERGUS	Looka mate, I've travelled the length and breadth of Ireland and never had to walk more than a couple of miles. (*lifts thumb*) Beats shank's mare, that does.
JOE	It'd be good to see a bit of the country alright.
FERGUS	Go where you like, when you like. Good grub on the farms. All you want. You work a day here, a day there. If it don't suit we move on.
TOM	Yeh, like some tramp or tinker. That sort of life wouldn't suit you at all Joe.
JOE	I don't think I could do farm work Fergus. I'd like to alright but, well you know, lifting and things like that . . . . . .

132

FERGUS	And who says you'll have to lift a finger. Not when you're with Fergus, Amn't I strong enough to do two men's work and no bother
TOM	Look who's talking! He can't even do one man's work here.
FERGUS	I told you, mate, this isn't a man's job. Besides it's different when you're on the road. It's share and share alike. Nobody ever said Fergus didn't take care of his mates.
TOM	(*low*) Now Joe, like I told you I'll see the gaffer in the morning about you staying on here. You're getting the hang of it and tomorrow will be easier.
FERGUS	Woman's work!
TOM	Give it a trial for a couple of weeks. <u>Then</u> if you don't like it — and I'm certain sure you will — I'll see about getting you fixed up somewhere else in Dublin.
JOE	Yeh, maybe it'll be easier tomorrow. It's nice and warm down here anyway.
FERGUS	Too shagging hot. Takes all the energy out of you. That's why you're tired, Joe. But suit yourself. I'm used to travelling on my own.
TOM	And don't forget I'll keep an eye open for some place, say near Dollymount, eh?
JOE	And I could get a bike, eh?
TOM	Why not? (*to* FERGUS) You'd better pick up your cards tonight. We won't need you tomorrow.
FERGUS	That's what I was going to do. I don't need you to tell me. Hump you and your shagging job.
JOE	Let him stay, Tom. It's only his first day. Give him a chance.
TOM	He's not fitted for this work.
JOE	But he could settle in. He works very fast when he wants to. Faster than me. Maybe if I spoke to him?

133

TOM   No. Leave it be. He'll go, and good riddance.

JOE   (*pause*) Give him a chance Tom. I mean, he's good company, for us.

TOM   A bowsie. That's what he is. Nothing more.

FERGUS   Whispering again, eh? Well, it's no skin off my nose.

JOE   Would you not think of staying on here, Fergus? Say for a couple of weeks?

FERGUS   Not me Joe. I've a great life waiting for me outside. (*gestures*)

           The whistle blows

TOM   That's it. Knocking off time. (*to* FERGUS) You can go now. (*to* JOE) Let's make a cup of tea.

           Looks across at chute. There are two bags there.

        We'll get one hour overtime anyway.

           FERGUS *puts on his coat and cap and looks across at them.*

JOE   I can't tonight Tom. Thanks all the same.

TOM   What! Are you turning down the extra?

JOE   I'm not able for it tonight Tom. My legs you know. I'm a bit tired like.

TOM   Look, you sit down and have a cuppa. I'll carry on. When you're rested up a bit you can give me a hand. No rush.

           FERGUS *strolls back.*

FERGUS   Coming Joe?

TOM   He's not. We've overtime to do.

FERGUS   Suit yourself. (*to* JOE) I'm going up to the Labour tomorrow to see that pal of mine. If you come with me he can fix you up at the same time.

JOE   I'd be sitting. Is that right Fergus?

FERGUS   Gospel truth. Ask my pal yourself. I wouldn't take it otherwise. And then after that I head South for Kerry.

JOE   *(puts on coat and cap.)* I think I'll go now Tom.

TOM   Listen. I'll get a stool. One of them bar stools. It'll be just the right height. I know a feller. You could sit on the stool all day. No one will know.

JOE   I don't know Tom. Honest.

TOM   But we were getting on fine. I was going to take you up to the brother's for supper one night. Any time you liked.

JOE   I know Tom. I'm sorry.

TOM   And the zoo. You said you wanted to go to the zoo.

JOE   I do. We'll go together one day. I'd like that Tom.

FERGUS   Coming, Joe?

JOE   It's no use Tom. I told you. I'm not able for — a steady job. Thanks. Thanks for everything.

> *He walks slowly to the door. He and* FERGUS *exit.* TOM *goes back to the bench and sorts in a dispirited fashion. As he throws a rag on to one of the piles he stops suddenly and examines it. It is clear that he has put a cotton rag on to the wrong pile. He starts as if to correct himself and then changes his mind. Almost savagely he throws it back on to the wrong pile and continues sorting listlessly.*

END

The (15 Minute) Dogg's Troupe Hamlet
by Tom Stoppard

The first performance of *The (15 Minute) Dogg's Troupe Hamlet* was on the terraces of the National Theatre, South Bank, London SE 1, on the 24th August 1976, by Prof. Dogg's Troupe of Inter-Action, with:
>Phil Ryder
>Patrick Barlow
>John Perry
>Paul Filipiak
>Jane Gambier
>Katina Noble

An Inter-Action Production designed and directed by ED Berman

Approximate playing time: 15 minutes

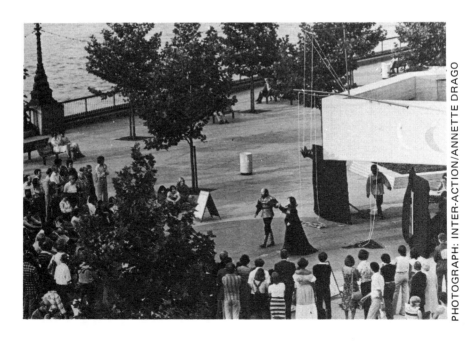

PHOTOGRAPH: INTER-ACTION/ANNETTE DRAGO

PROLOGUE

Enter SHAKESPEARE, *bows*

SHAKES For this relief, much thanks.
    Though I am native here, and to the manner born,
    It is a custom more honoured in the breach
    Than in the observance

    Well.

    Something is rotten in the state of Denmark.
    To be, or not to be, that is the question.
    There are more things in heaven and earth
    Than are dreamt of in your philosophy —
    There's a divinity that shapes our ends,
    Rough hew them how we will.

    Though this be madness, yet there is method in it.
    I must be cruel only to be kind;
    Hold, as t'were, the mirror up to nature,
    A countenance more in sorrow than in anger.

     Lady in audience shouts "Rotten"

    The lady doth protest too much.
    Cat will mew, and Dogg will have his day!

     Bows and exits
     End prologue

SCENE 1

     A castle battlement
     Thunder and wind
     Enter two guards: BERNARDO/MARCELLUS
              FRANCISCO/HORATIO

B/M Who's there?

F/H Nay, answer me.

B/M Long live the King. Get thee to bed.

F/H For this relief, much thanks.

B/M	What, has this thing appeared again tonight?
F/H	[1] Peace, break thee off: look where it comes again *(points off left)*
B/M	Looks it not like the King?
F/H	By heaven, I charge thee, speak!
B/M	*(points and looks left)* 'Tis here.
F/H	*(points and looks centre)* 'Tis there.
B/M	*(looks right)* 'Tis gone.
F/H	But look, the morn in russet mantle clad Walks o'er the dew of yon high eastern hill.
B/M	[2] Let us impart what we have seen tonight Unto young Hamlet'

> *Exeunt*
> *End scene*

SCENE II

> *A room of state within the castle*
> *Flourish of trumpets*
> *Enter* CLAUDIUS *and* GERTRUDE

CLAUD	Though yet of Hamlet our dear brother's death The memory be green

> *Enter* HAMLET

our sometimes sister, now our Queen
Have we taken to wife.
But now, my cousin Hamlet, and my son —

Footnote: In the extended play, 1 is spoken by MARCELLUS, and 2 by HORATIO.

139

HAM   A little more than kin, and less than kind.

Exit CLAUDIUS *and* GERTRUDE

O that this too too solid flesh would melt!
That it should come to this — but two months dead!
So loving to my mother: Frailty, thy name is woman!
Married with mine uncle, my father's brother.
The funeral baked meats did coldly furnish forth
The marriage tables.

HORATIO *rushes on*

HOR   My lord, I think I saw him yesternight —
The King, your father — [1] upon the platform where we watched.

HAM   'Tis very strange.

HOR   [2] Armed, my lord —
A countenance more in sorrow than in anger.

HAM   My father's spirit in arms? All is not well.
Would the night were come!

Exeunt to parapet
End scene

SCENE III

The castle battlements at night
Noise of carouse, cannon, fireworks
HORATIO *and* HAMLET *appear on parapet*

HAM   The King doth wake tonight and take his rouse.
Though I am native here and to the manner born,
It is a custom more honoured in the breach
Than in the observance.

Wind noise

HOR   Look, my lord, it comes. *(points)*

Enter GHOST

Footnote: In the extended play, 1 and 2 are spoken by MARCELLUS.

HAM   Angels and ministers of grace defend us!
            Something is rotten in the state of Denmark!
            Alas, poor ghost.

GHOST   I am thy father's spirit.
            Revenge his foul and most unnatural murder.

HAM   Murder?

GHOST   The serpent that did sting thy father's life
            Now wears his crown.

HAM   O my prophetic soul! Mine uncle?

                    Exit GHOST

            (to HORATIO) There are more things in heaven and earth
            Than are dreamt of in your philosophy.

                    Exit HORATIO

            Hereafter I shall think meet
            To put an antic disposition on.
            The time is out of joint. O cursed spite
            That ever I was born to set it right!

                    Exit HAMLET
                    End scene

SCENE IV

                    A room within
                    Flourish of trumpets leading into flute and
                    harpsichord music
                    Enter POLONIUS; OPHELIA *rushes on*

POLON   How now Ophelia, what's the matter?

OPH   My lord, as I was sewing in my chamber, Lord Hamlet
            with his doublet all unbraced, no hat upon his head, pale
            as his shirt, his knees knocking each other, and with a
            look so piteous, he comes before me.

POLON   Mad for thy love?
            I have found the very cause of Hamlet's lunacy.

Enter HAMLET, *exit* OPHELIA

Look where sadly the poor wretch comes reading.
What do you read, my lord?

HAM   Words, words, words.

POLON   Though this be madness, yet there is method in it.

HAM   I am but mad north northwest: when the wind is southerly
I know a hawk from a handsaw.

POLON   The actors are come hither, my lord. *(Exits)*

HAM   We'll hear a play tomorrow.
I have heard that guilty creatures sitting at a play
Have by the very cunning of the scene
Been struck so to the soul that presently
They have proclaimed their malefactions.
I'll have these players play something
Like the murder of my father before mine uncle.
If he but blench, I know my course.
The play's the thing
Wherein I'll catch the conscience of the King.

        Pause

To be, or not to be *(puts dagger to heart)*

      Enter CLAUDIUS *and* OPHELIUS

        that is the question.

OPH   My lord —

HAM   Get thee to a nunnery!

      Exit OPHELIA *and* HAMLET

CLAUD   Love? His affections do not that way tend
There's something in his soul
O'er which his melancholy sits on brood.
He shall with speed to England.

      Exit CLAUDIUS
      End scene

SCENE V

A Hall within the castle
Flourish of trumpets.
Enter HAMLET *and* OPHELIA, MARCELLUS
and HORATIO *joking,* CLAUDIUS *and* GERTRUDE

HAM   *(to imaginary players)* Speak the speech, I pray you, as
          I pronounced it to you; trippingly on the tongue. Hold, as
          t'were, the mirror up to nature

                    ALL *sit to watch imaginary play*
                    Masque music

          (to GERTRUDE) Madam, how like you the play?

GERT   The lady doth protest too much, methinks.

HAM   He poisons him in the garden for his estate. You shall
          see anon how the murderer gets the love of Gonzago's
          wife.

                    CLAUDIUS *rises*

          The King rises!

                    Music stops, hubbub noise starts

          What, frighted with false fire?

                    Exit, CLAUDIUS; *re-enters at side as* POLONIUS

ALL   Give o'er the play.

HAM   Lights! Lights! Lights! I'll take the ghost's word for a
          thousand pounds!

                    Exeunt ALL *except* POLONIUS

POLON   *(standing at side)* He's going to his mother's closet.
          Behind the arras I'll convey myself to hear the process.

                    End scene

SCENE VI

The Queen's apartment
POLONIUS *slips behind the arras as it is raised*
Lute music
Enter HAMLET *and* GERTRUDE

HAM   Now Mother, what's the matter?

GERT   Hamlet, thou hast thy father much offended.

HAM   Mother, you have my father much offended *(holds her)*.

GERT   What wilt thou do? Thou wilt not murder me?
        Help! Help! Ho!

POLON   *(behind arras)* Help!

HAM   How now? A rat? *(stabs* POLONIUS*)* Dead for a ducat,
        dead!

GERT   O me, what hast thou done?

HAM   Nay, I know not.

GERT   Alas, he's mad.

HAM   I must be cruel only to be kind. Good night, Mother.

                Exit HAMLET *dragging* POLONIUS
                Exit GERTRUDE, *sobbing*
                Drop arras
                End scene.

SCENE VII

                Another room in the castle
                Flourish of trumpets
                Enter CLAUDIUS *and* HAMLET

CLAUD   Now, Hamlet, where's Polonius?

HAM   At supper.

CLAUD   Hamlet, this deed must send thee hence.
Therefore prepare thyself,
Everything is bent for England.

> *Exit* HAMLET

And England, if my love thou hold'st at aught,
Thou mayst not coldly set our sov'reign process,
The present death of Hamlet. Do it, England!

> *Exit* CLAUDIUS
> *End scene*

INTERLUDE

> *At sea*
> *Sea music*
> *Enter* HAMLET *on parapet, swaying as if on ship's*
> *bridge*
> *End sea music*
> *Exit* HAMLET
> *End interlude*

SCENE VIII

> *Yet another room in the castle*
> *Flourish of trumpets*
> *Enter* CLAUDIUS *and* LAERTES

LAERT   Where is my father?

CLAUD   Dead

> *Enter* OPHELIA *in mad trance, singing*
> *Lute music*

OPH   They bore him barefaced on the bier,
Hey nonny, nonny, hey nonny.
And on his grave rained many a tear . . . . .

LAERT   O heat dry up my brains — O kind Sister,

> OPHELIA *falls to ground*

Had'st thou thy wits, and did'st persuade revenge
It could not move thus.

CLAUD   And where the offence is, let the great axe fall.

> *Exit* CLAUDIUS *and* LAERTES
> *Gravestone rises to hide* OPHELIA
> *Bell tolls four times*
> *End scene.*

SCENE IX

> *A churchyard*
> *Enter* GRAVEDIGGER *and* HAMLET

HAM   Ere we were two days old at sea, a pirate of very
          warlike appointment gave us chase. In the grapple I
          boarded them. On the instant they got clear of our ship;
          so I alone became their prisoner. They have dealt with
          me like thieves of mercy.

GRAVE   What is he that builds stronger than either the mason,
          the shipwright or the carpenter?

HAM   A gravemaker. The houses he makes will last till
          Doomsday.

> GRAVEDIGGER *gives skull to* HAMLET

          Whose was it?

GRAVE   This same skull, Sir, was Yorick's skull, the King's jester.

HAM   Alas, poor Yorick, *(returns skull to* GRAVEDIGGER*)*
          But soft — that is Laertes *(withdraws to side)*.

> *Enter* LAERTES

LAERT   What ceremony else?
          Lay her in the earth,
          And from her fair and unpolluted flesh
          May violets spring. I tell thee, churlish priest

> *Enter* CLAUDIUS *and* GERTRUDE

          A ministering angel shall my sister be
          When thou liest howling.

HAM   *(offstage)* What, the fair Ophelia?

LAERT	O treble woe. Hold off the earth awhile, Till I have caught her once more in my arms.
HAM	*(re-entering acting area)* What is he whose grief bears such an emphasis? This is I, Hamlet the Dane!
LAERT	The devil take they soul.

They grapple

HAM	Away thy hand!

CLAUDIUS *and* GERTRUDE *pull them apart*

CLAUD GERT	Hamlet! Hamlet!
HAM	I loved Ophelia. What wilt thou do for her?
GERT	O he is mad, Laertes!

Exit CLAUDIUS, GERTRUDE *and* LAERTES

HAM	The cat will mew, and dog will have his day!

Exeunt
 Drop gravestone
 End scene

SCENE X

A Hall in the castle
 Flourish of trumpets
 Enter HAMLET

HAM	There's a divinity that shapes our ends, rough hew them how we will. But thou would'st not think how ill all's here about my heart. But 'tis no matter. We defy augury. There is a special providence in the fall of a sparrow. If it be now, 'tis not to come; if it be not to come, it will be now; if it be not now, yet it will come. The readiness is all.

LAERTES *enters with* OSRIC *bearing swords*

followed by CLAUDIUS *and* GERTRUDE *with
goblets*

Come on, Sir!

LAERT   Come, my lord.

                   *Fanfare of trumpets
                   They draw and duel*

HAM   One.

LAERT   No.

HAM   Judgement?

OSRIC   A hit, a very palpable hit.

CLAUD   Stay, give me a drink.
             Hamlet, this pearl is thine, here's to thy health.
             (Drops pearl in goblet) Give him the cup.

GERT   The Queen carouses to thy fortune, Hamlet.

CLAUD   Gertrude, do not drink!

GERT   I will, my lord *(drinks)*.

LAERT   My lord, I'll hit him now.
             Have at you, now!

                   They grapple and fight

CLAUD   Part them, they are incensed.
             They bleed on both sides.

                  OSRIC *and* CLAUDIUS *part them;* OSRIC *exits*

LAERT   I am justly killed by my own treachery *(falls)*.

GERT   The drink, the drink! I am poisoned! *(dies)*.

HAM   Treachery! Seek it out.

                  Enter FORTINBRAS

LAERT	It is here, Hamlet. Hamlet thou art slain. Lo, here I lie, never to rise again. The King, the King's to blame.
HAM	The point envenomed too? Then venom to thy work *(kills* CLAUDIUS)
LAERT	Exchange forgiveness with me, noble Ha . .m. . *(dies)*
HAM	I follow thee. I cannot live to hear the news from England. The rest is silence *(dies)*
FORT	Goodnight sweet prince, And flights of angels sing thee to thy rest.

Turns to face away from audience

Go, bid the soldiers shoot.

Four shots heard from off stage
ALL stand, bow once and exit
END.

THE ENCORE

Stagehand enters with a placard bearing the
legend "ENCORE", parades across stage and exits
Flourish of trumpets
Enter CLAUDIUS and GERTRUDE

CLAUD	Our sometime sister, now our Queen,

Enter HAMLET

have we taken to wife.

HAM	That it should come to this!

Exit CLAUDIUS and GERTRUDE
Wind noise
Enter HORATIO above

HOR	My lord, I saw him yesternight — The King, your father.

HAM Angels and ministers of grace defend us!

     Exit, running, through rest of speech

    Something is rotten in the state of Denmark.

     Enter GHOST *above*

GHOST I am thy father's spirit.
    The serpent that did sting thy fathers life

     Enter HAMLET *above*

    Now wears his crown.

HAM O my prophetic soul!
    Hereafter I shall think meet
    To put an antic disposition on.

     Exeunt
     Short flourish of trumpets
     Enter POLONIUS *below, running*

POLON Look where sadly the poor wretch comes.

     Exit POLONIUS *running*
     Enter HAMLET

HAM I have heard that guilty creatures sitting at a play
    Have by the very cunning of the scene been struck.

     Enter CLAUDIUS, GERTRUDE, OPHELIA,
     MARCELLUS *and* HORATIO *joking*
     ALL *sit to watch imaginary play*

    If he but blench, I know my course.

     Masque music
     CLAUDIUS *rises*

    The King rises!

ALL Give o'er the play!

     Exeunt ALL *except* GERTRUDE *and* HAMLET

HAM I'll take the ghost's word for a thousand pounds.

     Enter POLONIUS, *goes behind arras*
     Short flourish of trumpets

Mother, you have my father much offended.

GERT   Help!

POLON   Help, Ho!

HAM   *(stabs POLONIUS)* Dead for a ducat, dead!

> POLONIUS *falls dead off stage*
> *Exit* GERTRUDE *and* HAMLET
> *Short flourish of trumpets*
> *Enter* CLAUDIUS *followed by* HAMLET

CLAUD   Hamlet, this deed must send thee hence

> *Exit* HAMLET

Do it, England.

> *Exit* CLAUDIUS
> *Enter* OPHELIA, *falls to ground*
> *Gravestone rises to hide her*
> *Bell tolls twice*
> *Enter* GRAVEDIGGER *and* HAMLET

HAM   A pirate gave us chase. I alone became their prisoner. *(takes skull from* GRAVEDIGGER*)* Alas poor Yorick — but soft *(returns skull to* GRAVEDIGGER*)* — This is I, Hamlet the Dane!

> *Exit* GRAVEDIGGER
> *Enter* LAERTES

LAERT   The devil take they soul!

> *They grapple, then break*
> *Enter* OSRIC *between them with swords*
> *They draw*
> *Enter* CLAUDIUS *and* GERTRUDE *with goblets*

HAM   Come on, Sir!

> LAERTES *and* HAMLET *fight*
> *Pause*

OSRIC   A hit, a very palpable hit!

CLAUD   Give him the cup. Gertrude, do not drink!

GERT   I am poisoned! *(dies)*

LAERT   Hamlet, thou art slain! *(dies)*

HAM   Then venom to thy work! *(kills* CLAUDIUS)
          The rest is silence. *(dies)*

          Two shots off stage

END

Hancock's Last Half Hour
by Heathcote Williams

The author has made free use of all available texts, including Hancock's own words; the preface by Peter Black to *Hancock's Half Hour*, an anthology of scripts, Woburn Press, 1974; *Tony Hancock* by Philip Oakes, Woburn Press, 1975; and *Hancock* by David Nathan and Freddie Hancock, William Kimber, 1969, Coronet Books, 1975; and acknowledges the help of Mal Dean, Peregrine Eliot, Dave Jarrett, Tuli Kupferburg, Roy Martin, Diana Senior, Peter Southcott, China Williams and Henry Woolf.

The first performance of *Hancock's Last Half Hour* was at The Ambiance Lunch-Hour Theatre Club at The Almost Free Theatre, London W1, on the 18th April 1977, with:
      Henry Woolf

An Inter-Action Production designed by Norman Coates and directed by Peter Southcott

Approximate playing time: 65 minutes

Copyright © Heathcote Williams 1977

All rights whatsoever in this Play are strictly reserved and applications for performance, both amateur and professional, shall be made to:
      ACTAC Ltd.,
      16 Cadogan Lane,
      London SW1X 9DX

PHOTOGRAPH: INTER-ACTION/ALEX LEVAC

*A room in a Sydney hotel. A bed, a supply of Vodka.
A large moose's head fixed to the wall. The floor is
littered with butt-ends and old copies of Australian
newspapers, Titbits and Reveille. A set of encyclopaedias
and Bertrand Russell's History of Western Philosophy. A
cuttings book under the bed. A large pile of papier mâché
hats. An astrakhan coat on a peg.*

HANCOCK *lies in bed wearing his clothes: jumper, grey
bags. Much of the time he holds the sheets over his head.
The bed is a womb with a view. There's a high-pitched
whining from the radio while the lights come up. The
radio then bursts into an early-morning programme
from a local Sydney commercial station, Hancock
fiddles with the volume control, turning it louder then
off.*

HAN Ba . . . ba . . . ba . . . ba . . . bee boom . . . *(breathing harshly)*
HHHHHHHHHHHA

His body heaves in a paroxysm of coughing

Ba . . . Ba . . . ba . . . bee. Boom . . . *(sits up and holds his
heart)* Thank you, thank you. *(talking to the moose)* If you
don't have enough passion, then your heart will attack you . . .
Shakespeare.

(To the moose) You must have been running very hard. I hope
the Aussies next door are happy with their daily view of your
bum.

*He pours himself a large Vodka, and throws piles of
hats listlessly at the moose's horns. None of them hits
the mark*

(muttering): There was a man once in Las Vegas who
practised throwing a key into a door until he'd got it right off,
then he'd gamble on it. Took Sinatra to the cleaners. He had
a rock on a golf course weighed once, then turned up a year
or two later with a band of well-heeled suckers. 'How much
you think that rock weighs?' Took them all to the cleaners. He
was right to the nearest ounce.

*He picks a bit of fluff carefully off his pullover then
looks at his glass*

This glass is dirty! *(shouting to the door)* Look, do you think you could go away and put some grease, some lipstick and a few more fingerprints around the edge and make a proper job of it?

(Staring at the glass) It's something to do with your hands. *(pause)* I used to do this all the time *(rubbing his lapel with his hands)*. George said: 'For God's sake stop doing that. It's very distracting for the audience. Put your hands in your pockets or something.' *(he puts his hand in his pocket, still twitching his hand)*. It looked very bad.

It wasn't George Arliss. And now. ladies and gentlemen, here's one for the teenagers. Where's the monocle? George Arliss. *(pause)* Rover! Woof, woof. *(pause)* What's the use.

(To the audience) Are you happy here? This used to be my ancestral home. In 1883 they built the West Wing, and then they built the East Wing, and the year afterwards . . . it flew away.

Welcome to Kookaburra Grove, Sydney.

Will you please imagine 15 flying ballet dancers, 78 trumpeting elephants, and anything else a scrounging stage manager can lay his hands on.

(Staring at an old Reveille) 'Tony "flippin' kids" Hancock shoots to star billing in his first outing with the Archie team. This man is funny. A slick script and smooth production marks this a winter winner as usual. Verdict: flippin' fine.'

Well, it's better than 'He looks like a St. Bernard who's lost his keg in a snow-drift,' or . . . 'Tony Half-Cock'.

What can you do?

What's this? *(he holds up three fingers)* It's this . . . *(holding up one finger)* . . . loaded.

How to entertain yourself for hours with no expensive props.

(Staring at the moose) Get out, Jimmy Edwards!

England. Still run by left-overs from the bloody World War Two clique.

Fucking Sid James: John Wayne with syphilis.

Oh yes, I've trod on a few faces on the way down.

Alan Simpson, Ray Galton. Tchah. You know one of the first lines they fed me? 'Call yourself a legionnaire?' 'Yessir'. 'Well, get your legionnaire cut.' Go back to the junk-yard.

I WANT TO BE OUT THERE ON MY OWN. Thousands and thousands of eyes, like frog-spawn . . . hatching. HATCHING ME!

Mike! Mike! Where's the mike? That's not his real name, that's his stage name. *(pause)* Imagine. *(Slumping slightly and screwing up his eyes).*

Did you know there's a special place in the middle of Hyde Park where people meet secretly to decide what kind of an audience they're going to be? They sit there for hours steaming in their plastic macs.

(To the moose) Have we got a seat? Certainly sir, you can have the first fifteen rows.

(Looking at his feet) I've got toes like globe artichokes. My feet have been put on wrong. They don't join the ankle right. I can feel them flapping like a penguin's. When I cross the lounge of a swank hotel, my feet come along with me. It's almost as though they were separate . . . not part of me at all . . . They flap, dammit. I feel I've always got the shoes on the wrong feet. Look at them! only useful for picking up nuts. If they're against you, your feet, you've had it. When I walk into the Dorchester they know I'm trying to impress somebody and they bloody well go off on their own. Feet are anarchists. But that's where the comedy starts, I suppose. From the feet up.

And what did J. B. Priestley say? What <u>did</u> J. B. Priestley say?

> *He picks up the cuttings book from under the bed, which has 'Tony' embroidered on it and is smeared with vomit, and reads in a Yorkshire accent.*

'Another despairing but different type is Tony Hancock, a very clever performer owing more to art than to nature. He comes on all smiles and confidence to recite, to sing, to dance, but is quickly reduced by the malice of circumstances to a gasping, pitiable wreck, his gleaming rolling eye pleading for our tolerance, for just another chance. This is all in a high tradition of clowning. Good clowns never try to be funny: they are very serious, but eager and hopeful creatures lost in a hostile world.'

To recite, to sing, to dance.

To recite! To sing! And now I'd like to sing you a little toon, a toon which we recorded over there *(American accent)* and would like to bring over here from over there to over here *(eyes rolling)* our latest record which should have been a hit but they forgot to drill a hole in the middle, a little toooooooooon . . toooooooooon . . .

A dance! Socrates said: 'Never trust a man who does not dance, never trust a man who does not prance.' *(he bobs around)* My bloody feet. Look at them. It's permanently a quarter to three. *(crooning)* Time . . . time . . . time is on my side.

And what about the recitation I hear you asking? *(composing himself into a Shakespearian stance)* Once more into the breach dear friends, or close the wall up with our English dead! *(aside)* omelette, the Danish Egg Head. In peace there's nothing so becomes a man as modest stillness and humility. Stillness and humility or not to be. That is the question. Whether 'tis nobler in the mind to suffer the slings *(mimes)* and arrows *(mimes)* of outrageous fortune oooorrrrrrr to take arms *(spreading his arms)* against a sea *(miming the hornpipe dance)* of troubles . . . *(pause)* I look like a lesbian.

Could Lorry Oliver fill the London Palladium? What a load of old cobblers. *(more Vodka, and then laughing hysterically)* TO BE . . . IS BETTER THAN NOT TO BE . . . THAT IS THE ANSWER.

(Quietly) It's a game, ennit?

I just want to thank you all for coming tonight. I want to thank Abdullah for the fags, and Kayser Bondor for the socks. Frank Sinatra for the boots which are killing me, and are going back, and I want to thank the police for controlling the crowds . . . inside the theatre.

Stone me.

Americans don't understand expressions like that. Stone me. Can you imagine? I couldn't imagine it, but there I was, on my way to becoming an international star. I went to see Stan Laurel. Did you know he didn't get a penny for any of the repeats? Another genius who got screwed up the wrong orifice. But he said to me: Stone me? what does that mean? if you want to become an international star, cut out the slang. He was on his death-bed.

When he was eighty-five, he went to Hardy's funeral, with all the other comics. They were gathered around the grave. Laurel was there. Over eighty, pretty crotchety. Some bright spark looks up at him and says: Hardly seems worth going home, does it?

Americans. You know what? They changed the title of my film The Rebel to Call Me Genius. Asking for trouble . . . *(whinging New York accent)* 'Why are you destroying yourself Mr. Hancock, do you really need all that vodka Mr. Hancock? It'll affect your timing, Mr. Hancock.'

CALL ME GEEENIUS WOMAN! Rub me three times and I'll turn into a bottle.

Stone me.

What is laughter?

The one thing that separates man from beast, said Dr. Johnson, who'd never heard of hyenas, and what do they laugh about? Death. They can't keep off the subject.

Ha. Remember Arthur Miller? He was asked if he was coming to Marilyn Monroe's funeral. 'Why? Will she be there?'

And old George the Fifth. Oh yes. When he was on his death-bed they said to him: Look, you get better and we'll take you to Bognor to recuperate. 'Bugger Bognor,' he said and snuffed it.

I performed there you know. Windsor Castle. A private viewing. By invitation. *(pause)* One clap the whole show. A one-handed clap, lightly on the end of a crossed knee. Hello, hello, hello, I said, my goodness, you must be the person who got my blood transfusion.

What a collection, eh? She'd only recognise a punch line if it was on a lead or ate hay.

(Mock lecture) Laughter is a language, invented on condition that there would be no dictionaries. Of laughter. It's all in Desperanto. But I made it. What did I make? 'Hancock! It's Tony Hancock! Go on Tone, say something funny.' Hundreds of people who think you're a taxi.

> *Drinks.*

I can see it now, plain as eggs. A jar of dusty daffs, and a rough-hewn stone bearing the legend: he came, he went, and in between . . . nothing.

This is your life. A slim volume indeed.

(Gets back into bed, pulling the sheets across) Is this the right position for a distinguished young fart? Let the peacock show its feathers. GET UP! What's the matter with you? We're turning back to Idlewild with mechanical trouble. *(Sitting up and pulling the sheet back)* Do you know that those tall, square-jawed cool-eyed aircraft captains they have on the airlines . . . they're just a front! They get them from a theatrical agency to settle your nerves. After welcoming you aboard they piss off to the next plane to do the same thing, and then they hoist a red-eyed, unshaven, fat, perspiring creature in crumpled dungarees struggling into the pilot's seat . . .

Fat, perspiring. *(looking at himself, wiping his face with a handkerchief)* Do they make these in white? . . . red-eyed . . . arsehole.

(Bending over) Are you there arsehole? We've got someone here who needs to use you in a disappearing act.

> *He gets out of bed.*

Now who amongst us remembers Clapham and Dyer in 'A Spot of Trouble' and The Two Live Wires, or Stainless Stephen the Semi-Colon? or the Vampire? sawing people in half using a real buzz-saw. Piles of innards flying into the flies. Oodles of offal. His patter only consisted of one line: THIS MAN MUST BE IN LEAGUE WITH THE DEVIL!

> *Black-out.*
> *Lights up.*

HAN   *(looking groggy and reaching for his Vodka glass):* That was
my black-out, not yours.

(Melodramatic, music-hall gestures) Ah, what is man?
Wherefore does he why, whence does he wince, and whither
does he wither?

An archaeologist. A geologist. That should have been it. A job
where you can trace things back to their origins. Where you can
get to the roots of things.

Pause.

Mr. Showbusiness . . . born in a trunk, will now regale you with
a little lightly exaggerated, but teasingly tawdry tale of his
initiation into the world of the farceur, the motley fool, the
chaffing japer, the wearer of the cap and bells, the équivôque,
the calembour, the scintillating jokesmith and jesting witworm
who sets the table in a roar, and lays them in the aisles.
(slipping into Robert Newton) Arrgh, Jim Lad! Vogue la galère!
Vive la bagatelle!

I shall skip my gory genesis and let the camera lingeringly pan
in to my first memory: with huge globs of vaseline liberally
daubed around the edge of the lens to indicate passage of time.

Jack Hancock, my father, A tall spiral shaped laundry basket.
A cab. We all get inside.

Suddenly Jack flips the lid off it, and says to me in a stage
whisper: 'It's gone again.'

'It hasn't has it?' I'm nudged and prompted to say in mock
alarm.

'It has,' says Jack. 'Quick, get the flute and play it, otherwise
we'll never get it back in the basket.'

The driver goes white, and tries to keep his eyes on the road
and looks around the cab at the same time. Finally he pulls up:
'EITHER YOU GET THAT SNAKE INTO THE BASKET OR
WE DON'T BUDGE ANOTHER INCH'.

It takes a long time for my dad to convince the driver that
there's no snake.

No snake. *(muttering)* And no punchline either.

Or was there. *(lying back on the bed)* I was a spunky lad. Yes. There was a snake in the garden all right.

(Touching his crotch lightly) No more now . . .

(looking down at his crotch) Come on out Charlie Kong, we know you're in there.

(Leaping up) Of course there's more now. More where it all comes from. HANCOCK! Ring your wives. Ring Cecily. Ring Freddie.

(Lying back) Ah sod it.

(Looking at his crotch again) What does come out of there? Eh? It's a psychedelic that's it! It's a <u>psychedelic</u>.

That's the answer. That accounts for it all . . . and men beat their wives to try and get it back.

(Morosely) I beat Cecily. I beat up Freddie.

I beat her <u>down.</u> *(he kneels down and prays)*

Dear Bertrand Russell, I know . . . I, Anthony Aloysius St. John Hancock, know that despite your philosophical objections that you are out there listening to me.

I would like to tell you that in this room there is a potted plant which I am finding it very hard to persuade to garrotte me at any given moment.

This is a coffee bar, yours Hancock.

> *Pointing at his body, with splayed hands and a look of horror.*

YOU'RE ALL BLEEDING MAD! All of you! Arms, legs, biceps, bicuspids.

I look like a bloody big bat. *(flapping his arms)* That's enough flying for one day.

> *Wandering around the room and picking up a heavy volume.*

'A clown is essentially a solitary man. He may work as part of a team for a time but his destiny and his need is to stand in front of an audience alone and say, in effect, "Look at me, I am absurd. I am you. Laugh." '

Ha . . . ha . . . ha . . . *(metronomically)*.

Deep breathing in morse code.

I've been into it all. This . . . secular ectoplasm called laughter. This heroin! I've been into it all, much deeper than that. It's a form of thoracic epilepsy, cured by a poke in the eye with a wet stick.

A joke is a little revolution, said George Orwell the notorious maligner of pigs.

Cracking a joke . . . Cracking it. A joke's a firework. A machine-gun bullet.

They're born of . . . *(woman's voice)* 'Yes, Tony we've heard it all before. They're born of frustration *(beating chest)* and despair *(pulling his hair)* and loneliness *(looking doleful)*. Your jokes Tony . . . just your fucking jokes.

Ah, belt up inner voice. *(drinking)*.

Was that my real inner voice? or just the outer layer . . . Exquisitely pickled.

Where's the book? ah, here it is. *(finding another text)*.

Sigmund Freud on Jokes. Entitled in the original Kraut: Sigmund Freud Up Witte and Up Yours', can you believe it?

Who knows his grandson? Dear Clement. *(laying aside the book)* Dear Clement, I have here in Kookaburra Grove, fifteen stone of kosher dog food *(rubbing himself)*.

Ladles and Jellyspoons, please do not be disturbed. This is the essence of humour: to perceive disturbance and then to realize everything is quite all right. Which leads to the following sound: Ah . . . ha . . . ha . . .

Yes? *(groping around for the book)* Sigmund, Sigmund? Where is the old gannet? *(finding it)* Ah . . . you see? Ah . . . ha, ha.

(Finding the text) 'Two Jews were discussing baths. One Jew said to the other, I have a bath every week, and the second Jew said: I have a bath once a year whether I need it or not.' *(looking up)* What a crafty little pleasantry!

(Putting his finger to his lips) The Great Freud speaks: 'The second Jew's insistence on his cleanliness only serves to

convict him of uncleanliness.' Analysis over. Amazing. What a mind!

Singing to the tune of What a Friend We Have in Jesus

What a Freud we have in Sigmund,
All our sins and griefs to bear,
What a privilege to carry
All things to Freud in his armchair.
Oh what Peace we often forfeit
Oh what needless pain we bear
All because we do not carry
All things to Freud in his armchair . . . *(dropping the book)* but how would he do second house at the Glasgow Empire? *(takes a drink)*

Looking up at the ceiling

Oh come on now, I've drummed up a bit of energy, is there anyone up there, or is it all a joke?

If it's all a joke, what are jokes for?

(Looking down again) This is ridiculous. I don't know any jokes.

Slumping. Looking around at the crap littering the room, and then looking up again.

IS THIS WHAT YOU GAVE YOUR ONLY SON FOR? HAVE YOU GOT NO TASTE?

(Kicking his way through the mess) A breeding ground for botulism. *(pulling back a sheet)*
(From under the clothes) Welcome back to 23 Railway Cuttings, East Cheam. I did everything in that bloody room except be indecent in it. I could tell you where every knot was in the wood. Where I burped. It was like a bloody death cell with an execution once a week.

Interminable evenings of wry shallowness. *(he seethes under the bed-clothes accompanied by a garbled collage of Hancock tapes)*

Springing up.

I've got it! I've got it!

A history of evolution from the first Plip to the last Plop . . . and just my face on the screen. One long mug-shot. One long ontological, epistemological, scatological, political and biological Rubber-Mouth. No sound.

(Getting up) He'll bite. He'll bite. He's got to. 'You can do anything, Tone.' Tony! You're as rare as rocking horse manure.

I might have to throw in my impression of Churchill as the Hunch Back of Big Ben. *(lurching)* Ding Dong Ding Dong *(in Churchillian accent).* We can ditch it later.

An hour!

Get them looking at a forked radish, a silent forked radish for an <u>hour.</u>

That'll get them.

They'll mutate.

'Let's hope the wind doesn't change, eh Tone?'

LET'S HOPE THERE'S A BLOODY WHIRLWIND, MATE!

Great!

What's there to eat. *(searching)* Man cannot live by booze alone. *(taking out a box of eggs).* One medium sized egg *(reading the packet).* Look at the size of it! One medium egg. It must have been laid at a séance.

(Still searching) Come on, I thought this place was meant to be posh. Grapes on the sideboard and nobody being sick. That sort of thing.

> *Flapping his hands like a penguin, opens another bottle. Broods.*

'That's nineteen and threepence on the clock, Mr. Hancock. By the way, you can take criticism? I must say that I thought your last show on ITV was rotten.'

'Must you my man? Well, let me tell you I think your driving is terrible.'

'Look here, squire, I was only telling you. There's no need to be personal'.

No need to be personal. Can you beat it?

Here's a tea-bag mate. Have a drink on me.

Pointing to his astrakhan coat on the peg.

Look at it. They've even ironed out all the curls. *(puts it in to the cupboard)* Night, night old son. Don't wet the bed again. *(looking around)* Why am I filling this bung-hole?

Pause.

(Picking up) Evolution . . . from the first plip to the last plop!

Yes. I know all the wrinkles. All the drenched quiddities clinging to this revolving sphere like leeches, and waiting for my tongue to lash them into life.

It's all in there you know *(pointing to a pile of encyclopaedias)*.

Never without them. They're home. Fuck the birds, fuck the booze. Sod the roof over your head. They're it.

Picking out facts from them as he builds the encyclopaedias into a kennel with a blanket for a roof.

Globodurenal ooze under the sea. There are twenty foot high worm casts made of the shit of the universe at the bottom of the Indian Ocean which must have been made by animals with rectums twenty foot wide. That makes the underground look pretty stupid.

The youngest recorded age for a woman to give birth is, wait for it, five. The little sods! That playschool.

And did you know, did you know there's a THING in space fifty light years thick. Now the distance from here to the sun is only eight light minutes. This thing is fifty light years thick How would you like that in your back-yard? Thank god we can still write to Marjorie Proops. Evolution. From the First Plip to the Last Plop.

Presented by the Lad Himself.

HANCOCK *gets inside the kennel of encyclopaedias pokes his head through the opening and starts mugging. A two minute riff of swirling eyeballs, nose-touching with the tongue, ear-wagging, scalp swivelling, and Adam's apple rippling. A semiological samadhi. Accompanied and orchestrated by the first bars of the music from 2001.*

At the end HANCOCK falls asleep, then wakes up and solemnly recites the following limerick.

There was a young man from Crewe,
who invented a new kind of stew
made of sanitary towels and elephant's bowels —
He looked very well on it too.

The kennel of encyclopaedias collapses — he rolls away from his demolished set.

Ladies and Gentlemen, I have it on no less an authority than Mr. Arthur Koestler that making a joke is a jump into space.

He hits the Vodka, starts twitching slightly, then mauls the phone.

What about Waiting for Godot then as a musical, eh Bernard?

Get your skates on, what's the matter with you? The steam age is past. It's all clockwork now.

All right, the thoughts of Chairman Mao. "There's unjust wars and there's just wars." No, he wasn't exactly Uncle Cuddles. We'll get Sean Kenny to do the sets. Hundreds of gapodas . . . gapodas — you know, cut-price pylons . . . and Spike. Spike can do the music. Ying Tong, Ying Tong, Ying Tong Yiddle Ay Aye . . .

No? Oh, copyright difficulties.

Well, here's one for you. A saga of that ever popular Viking folk hero, to be entitled the Wit and Wisdom of Adolf Hitler, lavishly studded with direct quotations from the Little Black Book: here's one for example. Table Talk, 1936. 'Water is unfrozen ice.' 'Toads are degenerate frogs.' Mein Kampf. Straight up. He wasn't just an ugly face you know. Amazing. I can see it now. The Wandering Gentile in thirteen parts. Its a chance to get your own back. Dear, oh dear.

(Slumping) It's all go, ennit?

Sudden sound of a pile-driving drill outside the window.

What? I'm having my teeth fixed. I'll call you back.

Where's he get the money? No, seriously where does he get the spondulicks? He's been following me around with that drill outside every hotel room between here and Honolulu. Streuth!

SHUTUP! If you don't shutup, I'll throw myself out of the window and kill us all! They murdered all the aborigines here, in cold-blooded blood, and the aborigines had perfect telepathic powers. They could tell when Sid was coming over from another village a hundred miles away and start cooking his favourite meal, a little wallaby steak, a bit of boiled fish, so that it would be done to a tee when he turned up.

He goes to the window.

CAN YOU BRING THAT BACK WITH YOUR RUBBISH?

GO AND PLAY WITH AN ELECTRIC EEL AND LEARN SOMETHING, YOU PARALYSED PRATT!

The noise of the pile-driving fades away.

Where was I? Honolulu. Yes, the Gretna Green of the Southern Hemisphere. Would you like to know how nature imitates art? I went to Honolulu to get married. Seriously. And to get a marriage licence in Honolulu Freddie and I had to have a blood test. 'Blood? You can have it if it's really necessary — plenty to spare of the stuff, oh yes, gallons of it, haven't we Frederika?' By the time they'd got the bucket out, my blood was swimming with rare and beautiful transparent Russian corpuscles *(indicating the Vodka bottle)* and they didn't want it. 'Listen my man, I came here in good faith to give you a spoonful of the best British blood, blood which has now become a symbol of détente, and if you don't want it, the best of luck. I'm going.'

A true story. VAMPIRES!

He slurps down some more Vodka, dropping a piece of ice in the glass and clinking it against the sides.

There's a sound. *(holding the glass to his ear)*

Sunday night at the London Palladium. Ladies and Gentlemen, welcome to this ornate garage . . . *(quietly)* Please turn on the exhaust and close the doors.

Melbourne.

He crawls around the floor on all fours, shouting at himself.

Rover! Woof! Woof!

(In an Australian accent) 'Get Off! Go on, fuck off the stage if that's all you can do. Sheister! Drongo! Bozo! Dirty pommy bludger!'

Hancock rears up and points at the audience.

LIGHTS! LIGHTS! POINT THE LIGHTS AT <u>THEM</u>! Go on, are you deaf in the flies?

POINT THE LIGHTS AT THEM!

All right then, eat shit. Twenty thousand flies can't be wrong.

'Booo Boooo. Get Off. SSSSSSSSSSSSSSSSSSSS . . . '

Ssss. The snake in the Garden.

Look here you convict rabble. *(lurching around with the glass)*

(Holding an imaginary mike). Not for nothing did I spend long years treading the boards as Jolly Jenkins coaxing small audiences into singing Every little piggy has a curly tail. I have ended up being photographed by Rembrandt.

Not for nothing, you unappreciative fools, was I Archie Andrew's private tutor for ten years. Imagine. How would you get on being tutor to a wooden doll? *(slipping into W. C. Fields)* Get away from me before I cut you down into a venetian blind. Take him away before I squeeze every bit of wood alcohol out of his body.

(In a ventriloquist's voice) A . . . V . . . C *(own voice)*: A . . . B . . . C . . . Come on, say B you idiot. No one'll see. We're only on the bloody radio.

And then *(slowly)* and then someone left him out in the rain, and his brain warped. *(crocodile tears slipping out into real ones)* Poor old Archie.

(Australian accent) 'Who gives a monkey's fuck who you are, get off the fuckin stage. Let's have Shirley Abicair. Come on Shirl.'

(Staring at the glass) Light me up. Light me up . . .

(To the moose) To absent friends, *(drinking)* chickety-snitch, and may some of them long remain so.

Australia. *(picking up a newspaper)* *(reading a small headline)*

'Mother of twins exhibits collection of lemonade bottles,' Can you beat it? Oh yes, it's all happening here.

(Picking up a letter) What a wonderful thing it is to have an agent. Did you know that Queen Elizabeth the First's agent was called John Dee, and he used to sign himself in secret despatches to her as 007. Straight up . . .there's nothing new under the sun is there?

(Opening the letter, and with Thespian drama) Now, what illuminated message is yearning to break forth from this recent occult despatch from my agent in Blighty yonder?

Ah, 'tis a clipping from that mighty Cerberus the Manchester Guardian. *(reading in a cut-glass critic's accent and then reverting to his own)* 'All we get is some tired clowning: the well known turns of the recent poor years of Hancock, the mock-Churchillian and pseudo-Shakespearian . . . Compére and stand-up comic is his least effective role. I suppose it is some personal ambition that he is determined to fulful. Remembering his team work with Sid James, with those scripts by Ray Galton and Alan Simpson (and even thinking of his very funny egg commercials with Mrs. Cravat), it is extremely hard to see why he should continue in this particular form of suicide.'

He looks into the mirror.

Good morning, Mister Frog.

(Placing the tips of his fingers together in front of his chest. Moving his palms in and out) Whatever's this? A spider doing press-ups in the mirror. *(he gives a clogged laugh)*

Did you know that toads can fuck for twenty-four hours without a single break?

(He places his hands over his face, then parts them in the middle) Draw the curtains. Rise and shine!

It's the lad himself.

He pulls his shirt open: vomit and bloodstains

On the side table is a large bottle of pills: amylobarbitone. He pours them into his hand, sits down on the floor and plays jacks with them.

GOD! Make it worse! Go on, show a leg. Make it worse. Show yourself up.

'Any last requests, Mr. Hancock, before we . . . we . . . er . . .'

'Yes, warder. Yes, thank you very much. How kind. I'd like to sing a song if I may.'

'Ah, I have some musical skills, maybe I could accompany you on the kazoo. What is the title of the piece?'

'It is called: Four hundred and forty-three million, six hundred and fifty-five thousand, seven hundred and twenty-three green bottles hanging on the wall.'

I'm funny.

I'm not funny.

I'm funny.

He swallows the pills and writes.

'Mum. I'm sorry to cause you any more grief than you've had already. The soul is indestructible. Bill, your friend the medium will understand. This is quite rational. There was nothing left to do.'

He lies down.

Do you know, I feel strangely cleansed.

I'm bursting out all over. *(swigging the rest of the Vodka in stark gulps)* Jesus, Mary and Joseph and the Trinity Tiller Girls. . .

Looking up.

There's not a clown in the sky.

Black out

HAN   That was yours.

END

The Irish Hebrew Lesson
by Wolf Mankowitz

The first performance of *The Irish Hebrew Lesson* was at The Ambiance Lunch-Hour Theatre Club at The Almost Free Theatre, London W1, in association with The Ben Uri Theatre Club, later called Jewish Living Theatre, on the 22nd January 1978, with:
>Leonard Fenton
>Patrick Drury
>Michael Low
>Patrick Connor

An Inter-Action Production designed by Norman Coates and directed by ED Berman

Approximate playing time: 40 minutes

The large attic room of a decaying eighteenth
century house in Cork. The room has been laid
out roughly as the interior of a synagogue, with a
raised platform with a piece of baluster around its
centre, chairs and benches at present disarranged
around it, and a large wardrobe with an embroidered
cloth hanging on it facing us and being used as the
Ark of the Law.

An elderly MAN, *bearded, wearing a skullcap and a*
huge praying shawl, studies concentratedly at the
lectern on the platform. He might be praying, but
actually he is learning the Irish for numbers and
certain essential phrases, translating them from his
native Yiddish into the English of the text books
before him, and then into Irish. He has lived in Cork
for 20 years.

From the streets outside, the sounds of firing,
occasional shouts, and boots running over the cobbles
to all of which he does not react.

The year: 1921. The time: very late on a mild Friday
night.

MAN   Yedes schtick kost sechs pennes, odder zwei far zehn pennes.
A spezeeler preis. The price is six pennies each, or two for
tenpence, a special price. Sé réal an ceann an praghas, nó dhá
cheann ar deich pingin, praghas speisialtá.

Eer kennt meer bezollen zwei pennes a vokh. I can collect two
pence vickler. Is feidir liom dhá phingin do bhailiú go luath.

De zeidene shall kost drei pennes. Is gemucht von indishen zeic
The silk scarf is three pence. It's an Indian scarf. Tá trí pingin
ar an scairf síodach. San Ind a demeadh an scairf síudach sim.

Hoizen, was far a greis? Zocken, shvarts odder veiss,
emessdicker boimvol, a penneh mit a halleb yede por.
Trousers, what size? Stockings, black or white, pure cotton,
three halfpence a pair. Brístí, cén tómhas? Stocaí, dubh nó
bán? Fíor cadás, trí leath-phingin an peidhre.

While he studies, a BOY *has entered the open attic*
window silently, and stands frozen, a pistol in his
hand trained upon the MAN. *The sounds from the*
street are nearer and finally disturb him.

How can I study with such a ferkukte noise? *(he shouts)*
Let innocent people sleep! Let a man do his study in
peace! Cossacks!

> *He gets up to close the window. As he does so the
> BOY draws back into the shadows.*

(muttering) Chazerim! Pigs! Mummzerin! Bastards! Black and
brown bastards! Bastards! Just a minute *(he checks in the
vocabulary he holds in his hands — reading)* Bastards. Where's
bastards. Mummzerim. *(looks for "bastards" but can't find it)*
Illegitimate maybe. Ille-git-i-mate. Yes! Bithiunaigh. Good.
(he shouts) Bithiunaigh!

BOY	*(with a Cork accent)* Quiet! Call them and you are a dead man.
MAN	Who said that?

> *The BOY emerges. He is very young, in nondescript
> clothes, his face pale, ascetic, that of a novitiate of
> religion or revolution.*

BOY	Quiet!
MAN	*(surprised)* What?
BOY	Call them and you're a dead man.
MAN	*(frightened)* Why should I call? You're a burglar.
BOY	Keep quiet.
MAN	That's a gun?
BOY	You're alone?
MAN	Up here I'm alone, except for you.
BOY	Below?
MAN	Only my family sleeping. I'll turn up the other lights.

BOY	Leave it! Draw the curtain.
MAN	Alright, alright. I'll leave it. I'll draw the curtain. *(he shrugs, draws the curtain)* You're a gunman.
BOY	I suppose you could say I am.
MAN	So *(he turns)* you kill old men?
BOY	I do not.
MAN	So, put down the gun. It can go off.
BOY	*(listening)* Will you be quiet? *(opens the door and listens)*
MAN	What should I do, sing? I am only saying —
BOY	I don't want to frighten you.
MAN	Who's frightened? I'm too old to be frightened. I've seen worse with the Cossacks. The streets ran with blood.
BOY	I'll leave soon. Let me listen.
MAN	Listen, listen

> The BOY *comes into the area of light from another lamp in which his face shows fully for the first time, so as to reveal his youth.*

MAN	Tsk-Tsk. You're a young man, a boy almost.
BOY	Well, we're almost a young republic. What is this place?

> He looks around the strange room for the first time. The MAN *watches him as he takes in the unfamiliar details of a small synagogue.*

MAN	This is my stebl.
BOY	What? Up here?

MAN	A synagogue, my father built it with his own hands before he brought the family over from the old country. After all he couldn't bring the family to a place with nowhere to pray, you understand *(pause)* my father, may he rest in peace, he was a religious man. I myself, I'm a religious man. My son-in-law he is already just religious. So I keep the place still going. The less religious you become the more you need religion.
BOY	A Jew Church is it then?
MAN	*(patiently)* A synagogue.
BOY	A synagogue.
MAN	Correct. Not that we get a Minyan here very often, that's ten of us . . . *(The* BOY *looks round).* In the old days it was different, but now they have smarter places. Less religion more smart. Who wants to drag himself up here? But I keep it all the same. It's a place to get away to, for my lessons.

The BOY *is walking about the room studying the terrain. He opens the door leading downstairs.*

BOY	That's the only way out?
MAN	That's right, except for the window.

Curious, the BOY *steps up on to the Bemah.*

BOY	*(suspicious)* A Jew man? Here?
MAN	*(shrugs)* What can you do? We're a travelling people. I'm not exactly a Black with Tan!
BOY	I know about you.
MAN	*(curiously)* What do you know? Did you see a Jew before?
BOY	One came to our market.
MAN	*(interested)* Oh yes? Where?

BOY   *(on guard)* Why should you care?

MAN   Nothing, only if you met a market Jew I must know him.

BOY   I'm sure. You're a close lot.

MAN   What can you do? We're a small family.

> The BOY *laughs shortly with tense nervousness, he walks off the Bemah and moves round to look up at the Ark.*

There's something funny?

BOY   Fat as a synagogue cat, my father used to say.

MAN   *(puzzled)* A synagogue cat?

BOY   *(laughs)* Yes.

MAN   Who keeps a cat in a synagogue? For what? Mice?

BOY   Fat, my father said, from the great feast of foreskins.

> *He laughs again. The* MAN *is a little put out.*

MAN   Personally, I don't think it's very funny, but if you've got something to laugh about, laugh.

BOY   I think I'll stay here for a while.

MAN   Welcome. Take a seat.

> *He clears a space at the table and the* BOY *crosses to the table and sits down, suddenly overwhelmed with exhaustion.*

Yes. I know all the markets and all the pedlars, the Jewish ones. It was in the West, you say? Macroom?

BOY   Never mind.

MAN   Please yourself. You're one of those revolutionary boys?

BOY	No questions!

His face comes full into the lamplight.

MAN	Alright, you're a young angel of death. This is a holy house, so welcome, angel. Oy, you look tired to death, angel.

BOY	*(suspiciously)* Were you talking Irish before?

MAN	Go mbeannaí Dia dhuit! Agus go maire tú ar feadh céad blian, agus go raibh fiche mac and míle muc agat! May God bless . . .

The BOY suddenly made irritable by fatigue, stands up again.

BOY	What kind of greeting is that? Twenty sons and a thousand pigs!

MAN	*(proudly)* It's a little something I threw together myself. You think the customers will appreciate it? You see I like to go now to the far parts where no-one else goes. Beautiful. Quiet. But the trouble is everything is in Irish. No, I don't mean trouble. So I must make business in Irish. Dia dhuit. God be with you. Tá sé fuar. It is cold. Ach, tá sé tírim. But it is dry. Buischas le Dia. Thanks be to God! It's good, no?

BOY	*(surprised)* You're a queer one, you are.

MAN	I sell goods by weekly payment, what's called "a vickler". I'll take twopence vickler, understand? Tigir?

BOY	Tigam. But twenty sons and a thousand pigs! There's nothing wrong with our old greetings and our new ones. Céad míle faílte romhat and bás don seo'nín!

MAN	The first part I understand — one hundred and fifty thousand welcomes.

BOY	A hundred thousand.

MAN	Alright. For you, a hundred thousand *(he laughs)* you'll excuse a Jewish joke. *(pause; no reaction from BOY)*

177

What was the rest of it?

BOY   Death to the English!

MAN   A cholera on them, we used to say. Only then it was the Russians — the Russian Empire, and where's that gone? All these empires come down into the dust and then a little child walks on it.

BOY   Please God.

MAN   Now, that's a Jewish expression.

BOY   And Irish.

MAN   Why not? God is a marvellous linguist!

> The BOY *feels suddenly dizzy and holds on to the brass railing of the Bemah.*

You look pale. You look white as death. Poor young angel of death, sit down.

> The BOY *collapses into a chair, suddenly no longer on guard.*

BOY   I've been running all night.

MAN   I remember the feeling.

BOY   Is there anything to eat here?

MAN   If I'd known a guest was coming — *(he looks at the remains of his meal on the table)*

BOY   Or drink?

MAN   There's a bottle of Sabbath wine somewhere *(he searches the adjoining shelf and finds a bottle)* Ah — here. *(he passes it to the BOY)* Take some.

BOY   Not strong drink.

MAN   It's not very strong.

BOY	I've taken the pledge. I'm a Pioneer. *(he is self-consciously aggressive)*
MAN	When he's about to die any man is a Pioneer. You're excused. Drink.

> The BOY *puts the gun in his pocket, takes the bottle, hesitates, then drinks from it.*

	It'll do you good. That's nice. You put away the gun.

> The BOY *stops drinking and puts his hand over his pocket.*

BOY	Look!
MAN	Don't worry. It's still there. Here. *(he pulls forward a dish with fish)* There's a piece of gefilte fish still in the bowl — I brought it up for dinner — and chaleh — white bread.
BOY	That's fish?
MAN	Gefilte. Eat. It's Friday, isn't it?
BOY	Is that fish in the Jewish?
MAN	That's the best fish in any language. Here!

> He offers the bowl and the spoon, the BOY *doubtfully tastes the fish.*

	So?
BOY	Hmmmm?
MAN	Eat, eat.
BOY	*(tastes it carefully)* Hm!
MAN	It's good, no? My daughter made it.
BOY	It's not so bad.
MAN	It's sustained the Jewish people like manna in a thousand

desert lands. *(he watches the* BOY *eating)* I'll get you some more. *(makes for the door)*.

BOY   Stay where you are.

MAN   I'll stay, I'll stay. *(long pause)* You know something? — You're another one of us.

BOY   *(surprised, mouth full)* Us? Who?

MAN   Certainly, you're one of us.

BOY   Look — I'm no Jew-man, I'll tell you that much. Mother of God — us!

MAN   I remember. We used to talk about the world ahead — the one we would make — where all the Cains become Abels so they don't have to fight each other to death any more. Yes, my dear sir, the dreams of men don't change. The trouble is neither do the men. So the brothers still fight. Cain still kills Abel.

BOY   *(wearily)* Oh — what do you know about it? Jesus —

       Shots heard outside.

       They're still at it outside.

MAN   Sure, sure. They're still at it. And which one are you, eh, are you the Cain or are you the Abel? Aach — who can say?

       He turns wearily away as the BOY *starts up alarmed.*

BOY   Listen you.

       He grabs the MAN's *coat and turns him violently around to face him, made rough by his fears.*

MAN   *(alarmed)* What, what?

BOY   *(tensely)* Mind your own business do you hear me?

MAN   I'm minding, I'm minding.

BOY	Ye'll be putting some heathen Jew curse on me with all your talk.
MAN	A curse? How? Why? Why a curse, when we're sitting here talking like two civilised men waiting for a pack of wild animals to run past? Please, relax yourself — who will come here?

The activity outside distances again and the BOY *relaxes.*

BOY	*(laughs shortly)* Ah — it was nothing at all, ye stupid old eejit with all your talk of Cain and Abel and the Blessed Bible. It's bad luck, so no more of it, do you hear?
MAN	It's bad luck? The Book is bad luck? Silly boy, it's kept a whole people alive better even than the manna and in worse deserts . . . Even your people also.
BOY	It makes me nervous I tell you. It's like listening to the Christian Brothers at school. First the little bit of Bible and then the crack over the head with the old leather belt.
MAN	Am I a Christian Brother? And look — I wear braces. *(he shows them comically)*
BOY	*(laughs)* You're a turn alright!
MAN	Well that's how you sell socks, you know, a piece of good advice here, a joke there. In a country market you must keep the people's attention. Remember everybody is selling something. Can they buy from all? No. Some must win and some must lose. That's only human again, like Cain and Abel.
BOY	I warned you, now didn't I warn you just — *(he leaps up)*
MAN	Alright, alright, calm down my dear sir, you get so excited. It's bad for the health —
BOY	Did I not just tell you that all the Cain and Abel talk is bad luck? I told you that didn't I?
MAN	It's nothing personal I assure you. Just a general remark, what else? Look, Jews and Gentiles, in all the colours of

the rainbow, all of us, under the skin, that's what we are, Cain or Abel. Believe me, I know that.

BOY   You know? You know nothing man. Nothing at all. A lot of talk and blather, that's all.

        The BOY *has walked back to where he put down the dish of fish and now studies it for a moment.*

MAN   Of course you're right, what do I know, what does anyone know? You're still hungry? Please, finish it *(hopefully)* if you've got the time.

BOY   It'll be a shame to leave it and to go.

MAN   *(eagerly)* That's right! Eat, eat, you must get on your way.

BOY   Maybe I will. *(he picks up the plate and eats from it ravenously)*

MAN   Eat in good health. . . You know, it's a pleasure to see a healthy appetite. Me, I don't have an appetite any more. Once like a horse, now more like a mouse with indigestion.

        The BOY *laughs, his essential good temper restored for the moment.*

        Mind you, I'm the same man I was, I'm still as good as I ever was in the markets. Ask anyone. Oh yes, they all know me.

BOY   *(suspicious again)* They all know you?

MAN   What? No — only the people, the little farmers, who else?

BOY   Christ. You'll know my face. It's a mistake to stay here so long.

MAN   Me? With all the faces I see? Never. Look — I'll tell you, when I'm up in the hills somebody will say "Hello mister, I'm wearing your socks, see?" I can tell you from which batch the socks come, but the face — I've got a terrible memory for a face. Feet, yes, but faces, terrible. Now my brother — he was the intellect — what a memory! What idealism! What a revolutionary! He, himself, he made a complete revolution for the Russians, and what did they do, they shot him for being an Anarchist. That's what happens to your good revolutionary with the intellect and the wonderful memory for faces. Me, I'm not an Anarchist — I sell socks.

BOY   It's the filthy informers — he was informed on, you can be sure. Anyway it's us that's fighting for our freedom now.

MAN   Well, he was shot alright, may he find his place in peace.

> The BOY *puts the plate down and reaches for his gun again.*

BOY   How can I be sure you won't inform?

MAN   Careful with the gun for god's sake. If it goes off it can wake up the whole street.

BOY   *(desperately conflicted)* God — how can you ever be sure.

MAN   Look — what are you talking about informers here for — for what?

BOY   The country's crawling with them — who can you trust? Look — how did they know about us? How was it they were waiting for us? We ran like dogs. *(near tears)* Christ — I don't even know who's dead and who's alive.

MAN   Quiet, quiet, please, don't get so upset. There's no danger here, none at all, I assure you my boy.

BOY   Trust a Jew man?

MAN   Why not? Listen — you know we used to have eighteen blessings in our religion, the Shema of course, and eighteen blessings.

BOY   Oh, what are you on about now?

MAN   Listen, listen, you'll hear. We brought in another blessing, number nineteen, you know what for — simply against

183

	informers. I've already said it quietly a couple of times. You've got nothing to worry about.
BOY	A blessing against informers? It's a grand idea altogether — but does it work?
MAN	Jewish blessings are highly reliable. Good. You nearly finished the food. Soon you can get away from here.
BOY	Don't worry yourself about me, old man. *(pointedly)* Wasn't Judas himself a Jew-man?
MAN	And Jesus wasn't? *(the BOY turns away, conflicted still)* He'll look after you, don't worry — he'll —
BOY	*(angry and bitter)* What's he care for the likes of me? I'm as far from him now as you are.
MAN	*(studies him closely)* Did you kill somebody?
BOY	I told you, no questions.
MAN	Don't tell me. Who's asking?

> *The BOY eats the bread moodily, staring at it and breaking off pieces and chewing concentratedly.*

In our village once, when I was a boy, someone from my own family — also no names, no details, better you shouldn't know — someone killed a man. *(he sighs)* Killing people makes you sick. *(the BOY grunts)* Not that it's so difficult. It was a stupid peasant he killed. Poor, drunk. For him anti-semitism was a kind of business. A pogrom was a chance to improve his standard of living.

> *The MAN settles himself down on the seat opposite the BOY on the other side of the table.*

The boy who hit him didn't know he was hitting so hard. With an iron poker it was. His head was smashed in so what was the use of apologising? My father left after that to find a new home for the family. You know something? When he came first here he thought it was New York because the bastard in Lithuania who sold my father the ticket told him they said New York! Cork!!

The BOY *hardly listens to the* MAN; *eats ravenously*

Just making polite conversation. The fish is good, eh?

The sound of a patrol car passing outside. The BOY *starts, stops eating and looks up.*

BOY   They're back. I must go.

MAN   That's a good idea? Now?

They listen for a moment. The sound of a van passing.

They're gone.

BOY   Maybe they're searching the houses.

MAN   A Jewish house? What for? Downstairs is my daughter and her family, and downstairs again is the old iron, silk scarves and the socks. In the backyard is a horse and cart and more old iron. Why should they search? *(he listens)* They've gone. Mind you, the horse is an Irishman. I call him Cúchulainn because he's an old dog.

BOY   *(relaxes)* Your pronunciation's not bad.

MAN   Thank you. Go raibh maith agat. Aach! At my age I must give myself lessons again. My family for a thousand years are learning new languages, but this is ridiculous. Tá trí phingin ar an scairf síodach. Three pennies for a silk scarf.

The BOY *is now sufficiently relaxed to lean back and become involved in the game with the* MAN.

BOY   You're always selling something!

MAN   Why not? Tá trí phingin ar an scairf síodach — the word of God, a good silk scarf *(picks up a prayer shawl)*.

BOY   Cheannochainn í agas faílte, ach níl an trí phigne agam.

MAN   You would buy it with pleasure, but you haven't got three

185

pennies. Now, just a minute, this is a good opportunity for a conversation lesson! Come, sit here. *(points to seat next to himself)* Praghas speisialtá duit-se, a mhic, dhá phingin ar an scairf fíor síodach seo ón Ind. *(translates proudly)* A special price for you my son, two pennies for the Indian silk scarf.

BOY   That's very good, only you should say scairf fíor-síodach ón Ind — *(translates)* . . . pure Indian silk.

MAN   Aaach! It's an impossible language.

BOY   Not at all. No more than yours.

MAN   Mine? Which mine? Yasik czary e ich kasaki? Vilstu reden mummaloshen? What language is mine?

BOY   Say something in the proper Jew language then.

MAN   Vos fur a Yolde ich dau?

BOY   What was that?

MAN   That's Yiddish. I'll read something in Hebrew.

BOY   What's the difference?

MAN   What's the difference between Irish and English? One's a holy language and the other's for doing business. Here. *(he opens a book and reads from a Psalm)* Im esh-kachech yerusholayim tishkach Y'meenee tidback l'shownee L'cheekee. Im low ezkraychee im low aaleh ess yerusholayim al rowsh simchosee.

BOY   For God's sake!

MAN   *(patiently)* Now you try. "Im".

BOY   Im? Im is butter.

MAN   That's right! In Irish it's butter. Well, well, go on, Im esh.

BOY   *(curiously)* Im esh. . .

MAN   Ka-chake.

BOY   Ka-chake.

MAN   *(surprised)* It's marvellous the way you make a 'ch'.

BOY   It's a sound only the English can't make. I have an old aunt
             who says the Irish are descended from the ten lost tribes.

MAN   I don't think so. They couldn't have got so lost.

BOY   *(suspiciously)* What do you mean?

MAN   Try again. Im esh . . . Ka-chech . . . Yerusholayim . . .
             Tishkach . . . Y'mee-nee.

             > *He puts the book in front of the* BOY *and then*
             > *slips round on to the bench so that they are sitting*
             > *side-by-side. He points to the phrases on the page of*
             > *the book and says the words again. The* BOY *repeats*
             > *each phrase after him, showing a quick ear for the*
             > *language. It is an extraordinary moment, for seated*
             > *side by side, they look like a Rabbi and his pupil.*

             Good, good! You've got a good ear.

BOY   Thank you! What's it mean? For you a special price, twopence.
             (he laughs)

MAN   *(indignantly)* Certainly not. No business in Hebrew. It's a
             holy language — for prayers, for psalms, for poetry, not for
             selling socks. Except in Palestine. They're growing trees there
             and picking oranges all in Hebrew. A group from my village
             went, some boys with long side curls and a few girls with red
             handkerchiefs round their hair. And now they are speaking
             Hebrew the whole time they pick oranges *(he sighs)*. That was
             before the war.

BOY   The German war?

MAN   The Japanese.

BOY	When was there a war with them?
MAN	Once upon a time the Russians fought the Japanese. Before that they fought the French. They did it to keep the Cossacks in condition for the pogroms.
BOY	Is that so! And what was a pogrom for?
MAN	Ahh, there's a question! *(long pause)*
BOY	Why didn't you go yourself? To Palestine. With the girls with the red handkerchiefs?
MAN	Me? I don't grow oranges. I'm a city man. What do I need it for? I was a married man with a family and so I sell socks.
BOY	You city men are all alike. *(pause)* I'd like one now.
MAN	What?!! A family? A sock?
BOY	An orange. *(he starts)* What's that?

> *Indistinct voices from the street below.*

What am I doing talking here? Thanks for your fish and your wine. I must be away.

> *He goes for the window and stops on hearing voices. Voices continue from the street below.*

1st VOICE	You two, try the alley!
2nd VOICE	Keep both ends of the street covered!

> *The MAN and the BOY look at one another in silence. The BOY takes out his gun slowly.*

BOY	Keep quiet!
MAN	You think I want to draw attention?
BOY	Look. I'm going to have to shoot my way out. There's nothing else for it.

MAN	So you'll get killed for it.
BOY	I'll not be the last.
MAN	You'll be the last and the first. Whoever destroys a single human life it's as if he has destroyed the whole world.
BOY	*(impatiently)* I've no more time for your talk. Put out the light!
MAN	You want to draw attention? *(pause)* A minute ago you were like a small boy learning a lesson — now it's the gun again.
BOY	The gun is the only thing we have in the end.
MAN	Who knows the end? *(looks around)* Just a minute.
	He picks up a prayer shawl and puts it on the BOY.
BOY	What are you doing, for God's sake?
MAN	A minute, a minute! You'll be a better patriot if you're dead?
	He opens a drawer and takes out a skull cap.
BOY	What are you thinking about? Look, they'll never take me for one of yours.
MAN	You're one of us, remember. Try this one. It's nice, with a silk embroidery, from Palestine.
	He puts the skull-cap on the BOY'S *head.*
BOY	Are you making a joke of me?
	The MAN *studies him carefully for a moment.*
	Finish now, will you? I look ridiculous. *(he takes off the skull-cap)*
	The MAN *brushes the* BOY's *hair over his ears. Actually, the* BOY *looks very Jewish, except for the gun in his hand.*
MAN	There's something wrong. Of course . . . .

> *He takes a prayer book, puts it in the* BOY's *hand and takes the gun away.*

Now, that's perfect. Maybe you even look too Jewish. Just a minute!

> *He turns the book round the right way. It reads from right to left.*

BOY   Give it back here! *(he grabs his gun back)*

MAN   As you like. But it spoils the whole effect.

BOY   I'll keep it hidden.

MAN   A gun under a praying shawl! It's not nice.

> *He puts on his own prayer shawl. They now look like rabbinic soldiers prepared to face the enemy with their very own special weapon.*

BOY   *(grimly)* I'll try not to spoil it when I fire.

MAN   With God's help you won't fire.

BOY   You think God wants to save the lives of those bastards?

MAN   Let's just hope that God wants to save the lives of us bastards! Sit down! Read! Gods wants us to study, that's what. *(he shows him the place in the book)*

BOY   Jesus! More lessons!

MAN   The same phrase. Try it. You never know when it'll come in useful.

> *Sounds of men nearer outside. Then knocking on the downstairs door.*

BOY   *(desperately)* I must get out of here.

MAN   You'll never get away. Now again. Im esh-kachech . . . yerusholayim. Tish-kach . . . y'mee-nee.

> *He says each phrase slowly in Hebrew again and the*
> *BOY repeats it again after him.*

Good, good. Again. *(they go faster)* Im esh-kachech yerusholayim.

BOY   Im esh-kachech yerusholayim.

MAN   Tish-kach y'meenee.

BOY   Tish-kach y'meenee Christ!

> *There is a noise on the stairs outside as heavy boots*
> *approach. The BOY starts up from his seat and starts*
> *to raise his gun. The MAN puts his hand on his arm.*

MAN   Im esh-kachech yerusholayim tish-kach y'meenee . . . .

BOY   Im esh-kachech yerusholayim tish-kach y'meenee . . . .

BOTH   Im esh-kachech yerusholayim . . . .

> *The door is kicked open and two BLACK AND*
> *TANS enter.*

1st B&T   What the hell's going on in here?

MAN   Good evening to you, officer, or strictly speaking, good morning. In either case it's good to feel that a citizen's protected no matter what time of day or night it is.

1st B&T   What's this then? *(he looks round suspiciously)*

MAN   This, officer, is a place of religious worship and instruction, in short, a synagogue. It's not much but it's all we've got.

> *The 2nd BLACK AND TAN is roughly searching*
> *for arms, making a mess in doing so.*

2nd B&T Bloody Irish Yid!

MAN   *(pleasantly)* You put your finger on it instantly, officer.

1st B&T   What are you doing up at this time of night?

MAN   We are religious men, officer. What have we got to do?
            When we do not do business we study, and when we do not
            study we do business.

2nd B&T   Bloody yids! *(he studies the* MAN) D'you know, Charlie, I
            read a book once — give to me by a Sergeant-Major, who
            was a real bastard — but a good'un — caught one at Mons
            he did — and he reckoned this book was Gospel.

1st B&T   You read a book!

2nd B&T   No listen, this book was by their Fathers or someone and
            it proves, proves, mark you, that the bleedin' yids are all in
            this plot together with the Catholics, and the bleedin'
            Freemasons, all bleedin' atheists you see, and with the
            bleedin' international revolution and bloody international
            high finance. And these yids, they're gonna take over the
            bleedin' world. *(to* MAN) That's what you're after,
            ain'cha? You old bleeder.

1st B&T   Come on Tom. There's nothing here. They can have the bloody
            lot so far as I'm concerned.

2nd B&T   What's he then?

1st B&T   Typical yid, ain't he?

MAN   A country man, just arrived. Doesn't speak a word of our
            beautiful English language. *(to* BOY) Im esh-kachech
            yerusholayim. Right?

BOY   Im esh. Im esh.

MAN   Kachech.

BOY   Yerusholayim.

1st B&T   What did he say?

MAN   He made a blessing for you. He's a religious boy.

2nd B&T   Bugger his bleedin' blessing! Let's get on Charlie.

1st B&T	Just a minute. Have a look round. *(pointedly)* See if there's anything suspicious we ought to take away with us. Right?
2nd B&T	*(delighted)* That's right. These yids 'ave got all sorts of very suspicious gold candlesticks and all that kind of clobber, 'aven't they?
MAN	You are welcome to search. Any gold candlesticks we have got we are pleased to contribute to your noble cause. *(he looks to the BOY and nods)*
BOY	Im esh.
MAN	My friend agrees. He says help yourself to the gold candlesticks. Those are brass.

> *The 2nd BLACK AND TAN examines the brass sticks and throws them down disgustedly.*

2nd B&T	They are bloody brass! *(smiling)* Shift your arse, Sheenie, or I'll smash your yiddisher conk in.

> *The BOY looks down at the 2nd BLACK AND TAN, his eyes burning with hatred. Beneath the shawl his hand is on the gun in his pocket. The MAN hurries forward to get between him and the 2nd BLACK AND TAN.*

MAN	Take no notice of him, officer. He's a deeply religious boy. *(to BOY warningly)* Im esh kachech.
BOY	Im. Im.
MAN	I'll show you officer. In there, there are the scrolls of The Law. That's all. Nothing of value to a man like you.
1st B&T	Look at him, bloody religious maniac. And him — fat as a synagogue cat *(laughs)*

> *The BOY is seething, white with rage. The MAN puts his arms around his shoulder and guides him to one side. Then he opens the door to the Ark.*

MAN   Yes, It's very funny, officer. You see, officer, no gold —
only golden words. *(he smiles)* Amissa mashuner. Chup a
cholera du mummzer, bless you, sir!

1st B&T   Bloody unholy gabble! Come on Tom, let's get out of this
Jew shit-house!

A voice from below is heard.

VOICE   What the bloody hell are you two doing up there? Having an
orgy?

1st B&T   Coming right down, Sergeant-Major. Come on, Tom, for
Christ's sake! There's nothing up here.

2nd B&T   Might as well take this.

*He picks up the bottle of wine, takes a drag and
spits it out, spraying the MAN and the books.*

Bleedin'ell. What kind of Jew piss is that?

*He tosses the bottle behind disgustedly as they both
exit. The MAN listens a moment to the sound of the
descending footsteps, wiping off the wine from his
face).*

BOY   Bastards! Bithiunaigh!

MAN   At least they appreciate the jokes your father taught you.

*The MAN closes the door and sets about picking up
the books and refolding the shawls. As he lifts each
item, he touches it briefly with his lips, and wipes.*

BOY   *(with self-disgust)* The dirty, filthy, stinking, murdering
bastards! I should have shot them down.

*He throws the cap and the shawl off furiously. The
MAN calmly continues to tidy up.*

MAN   Sure. So the whole family would be dead by now. Perfect
dignity is a dead man?

BOY	We're different from you. We have a country to fight for. We have pride. We fight for our dignity.
MAN	*(shrugs)* Please yourself. But do me a favour, please don't fight for mine. I prefer to live and remember.
BOY	I'm willing to die for what I believe in. Remember that.
MAN	Well, that's brave, very brave. But from my life I can tell you that it's harder to live.
BOY	What's the use of talking? I must get on.
MAN	Anyway, don't feel too bad about it. You can die another night, if you insist.

A WOMAN'S VOICE *is heard from below.*

WOMAN'S VOICE	Father, are you all right?
MAN	*(calls)* I'm all right. The lesson is going perfectly.
WOMAN'S VOICE	They've gone.
MAN	*(to* BOY*)* Better wait another hour or two. The curfew will be over.
BOY	*(uncomfortable)* I must go while it's still dark. I want to thank you.
MAN	You already thanked me. *(indicates the Ark)*
BOY	It's an odd thing to find one of you on our side.
MAN	You're one of us, remember. We all want the same thing.
BOY	*(hesitantly)* Maybe I should tell you —
MAN	*(quickly)* Don't tell me anything.
BOY	You're right.

> *There is the sound from the street below of the soldiers and the patrol car leaving. The BOY and the MAN listen. Then there is a moment of absolute quiet.*

They won't come back this way now.

MAN   Maybe.

BOY   I'll be going on, then.

MAN   If you have to. I'll see you out.

> *The BOY is about to leave, hesitates and turns to the Ark.*

BOY   I don't understand you people. Weren't you even angry when they threw down your holy books?

MAN   Our holy books have been thrown down so often, they're used to it. Anyway, books are just books, only the words are holy. You remember? Im esh-kachech yerusholayim.

BOY   Im esh-kachech yerusholayim.

MAN   That's very good. Your accent isn't bad at all.

BOY   What does it mean?

MAN   'If I forget thee, O Jerusalem, let my right hand lose its cunning. May my tongue cleave to the roof of my mouth if I forget thee, O Jerusalem!'

BOY   I know the passage well. It's in our Bible.

MAN   Your Bible. I'm glad to hear it. So, be careful.

BOY   I will. I must get on then.

MAN   Remember, God loves a live man just as much as a dead boy.

BOY   *(smiles)* I'll remember.

MAN   Good boy. Maybe you'll be President one day. Lech Leshalom. Go in peace.

BOY   Beannacht Dé ort. May God bless you.

> *The* BOY *exits by the door. The* MAN *looks after him for a moment, then crosses to the lectern, talking to himself, and continues his lesson from a small book.*

MAN   The price is sixpence each — or two for tenpence. Trousers. What size? Stockings, black or white. The day isn't good. Níl an lá go maith. The weather is bad. Tá an aimsir go dona. The night isn't nice. Níl an oíche go deas. The morning isn't good .... oy.

> *He sighs deeply, suddenly very tired, and wipes the weariness from his eyes and forehead.* CURTAIN *as he closes his eyes and rests his head on the lectern.*

END

The Examination
by Harold Pinter

The first stage presentation of *The Examination* was at The Ambiance
Lunch-Hour Theatre Club at The Almost Free Theatre, London W1,
on the 12th March 1978, spoken by:
      Derek Godfrey

An Inter-Action Production designed by Norman Coates and
directed by Jack Emery

Approximate playing time: 15 minutes

Copyright © Harold Pinter 1963

Grateful acknowledgement is made to Harold Pinter and to Eyre
Methuen Ltd. for permission to reprint *The Examination.*

PHOTOGRAPH: INTER-ACTION/IAN STERN

THE EXAMINATION

A bare, curtained, room with no means of entrance or exit.

Dark.

Centre stage, a large table, behind which is a swivel chair with arms. The table bare except for a decanter of water and a glass. Downstage from the extreme right of the table is a wooden stool.

The only source of light is a shaded bulb hanging low immediately above the chair and table.

Blackout.

General lighting comes up to reveal a MAN *standing at the extreme right backstage. He walks forward to the edge of the table and nods acknowledgement to his silent audience. As he moves towards the chair and sits, the general lighting fades slowly until he is lit solely by the bulb above. He opens his notes, pauses for a moment, and addresses his audience.*

MAN   When we began, I allowed him intervals. He expressed no desire for these, nor any objection. And so I took it upon myself to adjudge their allotment and duration. They were not consistent, but took alteration with what I must call the progress of our talks. With the chalk I kept I marked the proposed times upon the blackboard, before the beginning of a session, for him to examine, and to offer any criticism if he felt so moved. But he made no objection, nor, during our talks, expressed any desire for a break in the proceedings. However, as I suspected they might benefit both of us, I allowed him intervals.

The intervals themselves, when they occurred, at whatever juncture, at whatever crucial point, preceded by whatever deadlock, were passed, naturally, in silence. It was not uncommon for them to be both preceded and followed by an equal silence, but this is not to say that on such occasions their purpose was offended. Frequently his disposition would be such that little could be achieved by insistence, or by persuasion. When Kullus was disposed to silence I invariably acquiesced, and prided myself on those occasions with tactical acumen. But I did not regard these silences as intervals, for they were not, and neither, I think, did Kullus so regard them. For if Kullus fell silent, he did not cease to participate in our examination. Never, at any time, had I reason to doubt his active participation, through word and through silence, between interval and interval, and I recognized what I took to be his devotion as actual and unequivocal, besides, as it seemed to me, obligatory. And so the nature of our silence within the frame of our examination, and the nature of our silence outside the frame of our examination, were entirely opposed.

Upon my announcement of an interval Kullus would change, or act in such a manner as would suggest change. His behaviour, on these occasions, was not consistent, nor, I am convinced, was it initiated by motives of resentment or enmity, although I suspect Kullus was aware of my watchfulness. Not that I made any pretence to be otherwise. I was obliged to remark, and, if possible, to verify, any ostensible change in his manner, whether it was outside the frame of our examination or not. And it is upon this point that I could be accused of error. For gradually it appeared that these intervals proceeded according to his terms. And where both allotment and duration had rested with me, and had become my imposition, they now proceeded according to his dictates, and became his imposition.

For he journeyed from silence to silence, and I had no course but to follow. Kullus's silence, where he was entitled to silence, was compounded of numerous characteristics, the which I duly noted. But I could not always follow his courses, and where I could not follow, I was no longer his dominant.

Kullus's predilection for windows was not assumed. At every interval, he retired to the window, and began from its vantage, as from a source. On approaching initially when the break was stated, he paid no attention to the aspect beyond, either in day-time or in night-time. And only in his automatic course to the window, and his lack of interest in the aspect beyond, did he prove consistent.

Neither was Kullus's predilection for windows a deviation from former times. I had myself suffered under his preoccupation upon previous occasions, when the order of his room had been maintained by particular arrangement of window and curtain, according to day and to night, and seldom to my taste or my comfort. But now he maintained no such order and did not determine their opening or closing. For we were no longer in Kullus's room.

And the window was always open, and the curtains were always open.

Not that Kullus displayed any interest in this constant arrangement, in the intervals, when he might note it. But as I suspect he was aware of my watchfulness, so I suspect he was aware of my arrangement. Dependent on the intensity of his silence I could suspect and conclude, but where his silence was too deep for echo, I could neither suspect nor conclude. And so gradually, where this occurred, I began to take the only course open to me, and terminated the intervals arbitrarily, cutting short the proposed duration, when I could no longer follow him, and was no longer his dominant.

But this was not until later.

When the door opened. When Kullus, unattended, entered, and the interim ended. I turned from all light in the window, to pay him due regard and welcome. Whereupon without reserve or hesitation, he moved from the door as from shelter, and stood in the light from the window. So I watched the entrance become vacant, which had been his shelter. And observed the man I had welcomed, he having crossed my border.

Equally, now, I observed the selected properties, each in their place; the blackboard, the window, the stool. And the door had closed and was absent, and of no moment. Imminent upon opening and welcoming it had possessed moment. Now only one area was to witness activity and to suffer procedure, and that only was necessary and valid. For the door was closed and so closed.

Whereupon I offered Kullus the stool, the which I placed for him. He showed, at this early juncture, no disregard for my directions; if he did not so much obey, he extended his voluntary co-operation. This was sufficient for my requirements. That I detected in him a desire for a summation of our efforts spoke well for the progress of our examination. It was my aim to avoid the appearance of subjection; a common policy, I understand, in like examinations. Yet I was naturally dominant, by virtue of my owning the room; he having entered through the door I now closed. To be confronted with the especial properties of my abode, bearing the seal and arrangement of their tenant, allowed only for recognition on the part of my visitor, and through recognition to acknowledgement, and through acknowledgement to appreciation, and through appreciation to subservience. At least, I trusted that such a development would take place, and initially believed it to have done so. It must be said, however, that his manner, from time to time, seemed to border upon indifference, yet I was not deluded by this, or offended. I viewed it as a utility he was compelled, and entitled, to fall back on, and equally as a tribute to my own incisiveness and patience. And if then I viewed it as a tactical measure, it caused me little concern. For it seemed, at this time, that the advantage was mine. Had not Kullus been obliged to attend this examination? And was not his attendance an admission of that obligation? And was not his admission an acknowledgement of my position? And my position therefore a position of dominance? I calculated this to be so, and no early event caused me to re-assess this calculation. Indeed, so confident was I in the outcome of our talks, that I decided to allow him intervals.

To institute these periods seemed to me both charitable and politic. For I hoped he might benefit from a period of no demand, so be better equipped for the periods of increased demand which would follow. And, for a time, I had no reason to doubt the wisdom of this arrangement. Also, the context of the room in which Kullus moved during the intervals was familiar and sympathetic to me, and not so to him. For Kullus had known it, and now knew it no longer, and took his place in it as a stranger, and when each break was stated, was compelled to pursue a particular convention and habit in his course, so as not to become hopelessly estranged within its boundaries. But gradually it became apparent that only in his automatic course to the window, and his lack of interest in the aspect beyond, did he prove consistent.

Prior to his arrival, I had omitted to establish one property in the room, which I knew to be familiar to him, and so liable to bring him to ease. And never once did he remark the absence of a flame in the grate. I concluded he did not recognise this absence. To balance this, I emphasized the presence of the stool, indeed, placed it for him, but as he never once remarked this presence, I concluded his concern did not embrace it. Not that it was at any time simple to determine by what particular his concern might be engaged. However, in the intervals, when I was able to observe him with possibly a finer detachment, I hoped to determine this.

Until his inconsistency began to cause me alarm, and his silence to confound me.

I can only assume Kullus was aware, on these occasions, of the scrutiny of which he was the object, and was persuaded to resist it, and to act against it. He did so by deepening the intensity of his silence, and by taking courses I could by no means follow, so that I remained isolated, and outside his silence, and thus of negligible influence. And so I took the only course open to me, and terminated the intervals arbitrarily, cutting short the proposed duration, when I could no longer follow him, and was no longer his dominant.

For where the intervals had been my imposition, they had now become his imposition.

Kullus made no objection to this adjustment, though without doubt he noted my anxiety. For I suffered anxiety with good cause, out of concern for the progress of our talks, which now seemed to me to be affected. I was no longer certain whether Kullus participated in our examination, nor certain whether he still understood that as being the object of our meeting. Equally, the nature of our silences, which formerly were distinct in their opposition: that is, a silence within the frame of our examination, and a silence outside the frame of our examination, seemed to me no longer opposed, indeed were indistinguishable, and were one silence, dictated by Kullus.

And so the time came when Kullus initiated intervals at his own inclination, and pursued his courses at will, and I was able to remark some consistency in his behaviour. For now I followed him in his courses without difficulty, and there was no especial duration for interval or examination, but one duration, in which I participated. My devotion was actual and unequivocal. I extended my voluntary co-operation, and made no objection to procedure. For I desired a summation of our efforts. And when Kullus remarked the absence of a flame in the grate, I was bound to acknowledge this. And when he remarked the presence of the stool, I was equally bound. And when he removed the blackboard, I offered no criticism. And when he closed the curtains I did not object.

For we were now in Kullus's room.

> *The speaker is still and silent for a few seconds. He closes his notebook, and as the general lighting returns, rises from the chair and returns to his previous position at the right hand edge of the table facing his audience. He nods in acknowledgement and turns to go. As he reaches the back wall —*
>
> *Blackout.*

END

Notes on the Authors

Wolf Mankowitz. Born 1924. Novels: *Make Me an Offer,* 1952;
A Kid for Two Farthings, 1955; *My Old Man's a Dustman,* 1956;
Cockatrice, 1963; *Penguin Wolf Mankowitz,* 1967. Histories:
Wedgewood, 1953; *The Portland Vase,* 1953; *An Encyclopedia of
English Pottery and Porcelain,* 1957. Poetry: *12 Poems,* 1971. Plays:
The Bespoke Overcoat and Other Plays, 1955; *Expresso Bongo,* 1958;
Make Me an Offer (musical), 1959; *Belle* (musical), 1961; *Pickwick*
(musical), 1963; *Samson Riddle,* 1972; *Stand and Deliver,* 1972.
Films: *Make Me an Offer,* 1954; *A Kid for Two Farthings,* 1954;
The Bespoke Overcoat, 1955; *The Millionairess,* 1960; *The Long and
the Short and the Tall,* 1961; *The Day the Earth Caught Fire,* 1961;
The Waltz of the Toreadors, 1962; *Casino Royale,* 1967; *The
Assassination Bureau,* 1969; *Bloomfield,* 1970; *Black Beauty,* 1971;
Treasure Island, 1972; *The Hebrew Lesson,* 1973; *The Hireling,* 1973.
Television: *Dickens of London,* 1976; *Extraordinary Mr. Poe,* 1978.

Frank Marcus's stage plays include: *Minuet for Stuffed Birds*
(directed by himself at the Torch Theatre, London), *The Man Who
Bought a Battlefield, The Formation Dancers, The Killing of Sister
George* (Evening Standard Best Play of the Year award, 1965),
*Cleo, Studies of the Nude, Mrs. Mouse Are You Within?, Notes on a
Love Affair, Blank Pages, Christmas Carol, Beauty and the Beast,
Anatol* (adaptation) and *Blind Date,* in addition to *The Window.*
His TV plays include: *The Window, A Temporary Typist, The Glove
Puppet, Blank Pages* and *Carol's Story.*

Harold Pinter began his career as an actor. He wrote *The Examination*
in 1954. His first major play to be staged in London was *The
Birthday Party* in 1958, followed in 1960 by *The Caretaker.* His
shorter plays, including *The Room, The Dumb Waiter, A Slight Ache,*
and the double bill of *Landscape* and *Silence* have been widely
performed. Most of his work for radio and television, including
The Collection, A Night Out and *The Lover,* has been successfully
transferred to the stage. *Tea Party* and *The Basement,* both originally
performed on television, were presented at the Duchess Theatre.
Old Times was in the Royal Shakespeare Company's repertoire at the
Aldwych. His screen plays include *The Servant, The Pumpkin Eater,
The Quiller Memorandum, Accident, The Go-Between, A La
Recherche du Temps Perdu* and *The Last Tycoon.* His latest plays, *No
Man's Land* and *Betrayal,* were first presented at the National Theatre.

James Saunders was born in London in 1925. His screenplay, *The Sailor's Return,* is currently being filmed with Jack Gold directing. He has just completed a four-part television series based on a novel by R. M. Delderfield for London Weekend Television. His stage plays include: *Alas Poor Fred* (1959), *Next Time I'll Sing to You* (1963 Evening Standard Most Promising Play award), *A Scent of Flowers* (1964), *The Italian Girl* (1967), *The Travails of Sancho Panza* (1969), *Games After Liverpool* (1971) presented at The Almost Free Theatre, *Hans Kohlaas* (1972), *Bye Bye Blues* (1973), *The Island* (1975) and *Bodies* (1977). He has written a number of plays for radio, and for television has adapted six stories by D. H. Lawrence and written three plays for the series *Country Matters* for Granada.

Norman Smythe was born in New York City, the son of Irish immigrants. He was sent back to Ireland at the age of three, returning to New York when he was sixteen. While learning to write he was, among other things, a seaman and a founder member of the National Maritime Union, and also worked in the theatre. After another spell in Ireland he returned to the US and became a sales engineer, at the same time publishing short stories and feature articles, and writing for radio and television. In 1962 he went back to Dublin and devoted himself to full time journalism. He then joined Radio Telefis Eireann where he is at present a script editor in the drama department. In addition to *The Ragpickers* — first published as one of *The Best Short Plays of 1973* in New York, he has had plays produced on stage and television, including *The Station,* presented at the Dublin Theatre Festival in 1967, and *The Prison,* which won a special award at the Prague Festival in 1970. Many of his plays have been translated.

Michael Stevens, a native of Stoke-on-Trent, saw his first play for the stage, *Have You Met Our Rabbit?,* produced by ED Berman at the Oval House, Kennington in 1970 with Prunella Scales and Robert Coleby in the lead. The play has since been performed in Edinburgh, South Africa and New York. A year later *Companion Piece* was produced at The Almost Free Theatre. *An Empty Square,* runner-up in the University of Wales Eisteddfod 1973 was later incorporated with *Office Party* and *Cleaners to the Duke of Edinburgh (By Appointment)* into a trilogy of one-act plays. His other plays include: *Green Stranger, The Dangerous Age, Slow Down You're Going Too Fast, Mr. Pinocchio, The Locusts,* written for the Northampton Festival of 1975, *Masterclass,* a radio play, *Solitary Confinement,* an entertainment in six scenes for solo actress with music by Alan

Gibson, and a full-length play for television, *The Caravan.* Michael Stevens is married, with two daughters and now lives and works in Manchester.

Tom Stoppard has written *After Magritte, Dogg's Our Pet,* and *The (15-Minute) Dogg's Troupe Hamlet* for Inter-Action. His *Dirty Linen & New-Found-Land* opened 'The American Connection: Part 1', an Ambiance Lunch-Hour season at The Almost Free Theatre. His other plays include: *Enter a Free Man, The Real Inspector Hound,* Evening Standard award winners *Jumpers, Rosencrantz and Guildenstern Are Dead* and *Travesties* (the latter two also won Tony Awards on Broadway), *Every Good Boy Deserves Favour* and *Night and Day.* He has also written for radio and television, and one novel, *Lord Malquist and Mr. Moon.* He began his writing career in journalism, working for the Western Daily Press and the Evening World in Bristol, and later as a freelance jounalist in Bristol and London. He lives in Buckinghamshire with his wife and four children.

Heathcote Williams is the author of *AC/DC, The Speakers,* a documentary novel about four Hyde Park orators, *The Local Stigmatic, The Truth Dentist,* and the orgiastic opera, *The Supernatural Family.* As a partner in the Ruff Tuff Creem Puff Estate Agency, which provides free accommodation for the homeless, he has been involved in various enlightened crimes, such as opening up the Palm Court Hotel for the battered wives and children of Chiswick Women's Aid and squatting the Albion Free State Meat Roxy, a former bingo hall in the Ladbroke Archipelago, where he organised free days and nights of nameless wildness. A volume of his essays, manifestoes and graffiti on God, Sex, Death, squatting, Beasts Liberation, Plant Lib., suing the Chief Constable of Windsor, etc., to be entitled *Severe Joy,* is to appear soon from John Calder. Mr Williams is currently editing *The Fanatic,* a paper of passion, with Richard Adams and John Mitchell.

ED Berman, MBE. Born USA 1941. Naturalized British citizen, 1976. Playwright: *Freeze, Stamp, Super Santa, Sagittarius, Virgo, The Nudist Campers Grow and Grow, The Alien Singer.* Theatre director: *Savoury Meringue* by James Saunders, *Piccadilly Capers* by Phil Woods, *Dirty Linen* by Tom Stoppard, *Samson and Delilah* by Wolf Mankowitz, etc. Theatre producer: 130 premieres for adults and 140 new plays for children. Created BARC — British American Repertory Company, 1978. Community artist: created Game Plays and Act-Ins for street theatre, Fun Art Bus, Fun Art Loo, Community Cameos, etc. Founded Father Xmas Union, City Farm Movement, Sports-Space (co-founder), etc. Educational film maker: *The Head, Two Weeler, The (15 Minute) Dogg's Troupe Hamlet,* etc. Publications: *Prof. R.L. Dogg's Zoo's Who I and II, The Creative Game* (in preparation).

About Inter-Action

Inter-Action is the umbrella name for a group of charities founded in 1968 by ED Berman to stimulate community involvement in the arts, especially through the use of drama and creative play, and to experiment in theatre/media and its social applications.

The work of Inter-Action is broadly divided into two categories — theatre and community work. The Almost Free Theatre provides a showcase for experimental film, music, poetry and arts activities, and is the permanent base for the Ambiance Lunch-Hour Theatre Club which presents at least ten one-act plays each year. Inter-Action theatre work also embraces Dogg's Troupe street and children's theatre, the Fun Art Bus, Community Cameo Agency for indigent writers (William Shakespeare and Edward Lear are the first clients and are now making appearances), Animobile — a farmyard-on-wheels using story-telling to bring children into contact with animals, and the most recent creation: British American Repertory Company (BARC), a trans-Atlantic company of British and Americans playing an extensive repertoire of children's and adult theatre in both countries and including Short-Cuts to Shakespeare.

The sixty members of Inter-Action work and live co-operatively in Kentish Town, London Borough of Camden. Their skills provide a professional basis for the community work which includes: a community resource centre (printing, video, etc.); an advisory service for voluntary groups; an alternative education project; City Farm I with its indoor riding school; and an inner city sports program — Sports-Space.

A list of publications from Inprint, the publishing arm of Inter-Action, is available on request.